SIS Volume XIII, Number 10

Creating the Post-Communist Order

Red Armies in Crisis

by Bruce D. Porter

foreword by Stephen Sestanovich

WESTVIEW PRESS * BOULDER, COLORADO

The Center for Strategic
and International Studies
Washington, D.C.

Library of Congress Cataloging-in-Publication Data

Porter, Bruce D.
   Red armies in crisis / by Bruce D. Porter : foreword by
Stephen Sestanovich
         p.   cm. — (Creating the post-communist order) (Significant
issues series, ISSN 0736-7136 ; v. 13, no. 10)
   Includes bibliographical references.
   ISBN 0-89206-175-8
   1. Communist countries—Armed Forces. 2. Europe, Eastern—
Armed Forces. 3. Soviet Union—Armed Forces. I. Title. II. Series.
III. Series: Significant issues series, v.13, no. 10.
UA15.P67 1991
355'.009171'7—dc20   91-4983
                                                                        CIP

Cover design by Hasten & Hunt Graphic Design, Inc.

WESTVIEW PRESS
Frederick A. Praeger, Publisher
5500 Central Avenue
Boulder, Colorado 80301

The Center for Strategic and International Studies
Washington, D.C.

Printed on Recycled Paper

Contents

About the Author

Bruce D. Porter is currently the Harry and Lynde Bradley senior research associate at the Olin Institute for Strategic Studies under the Center for International Affairs, Harvard University. He previously served for several years as executive director of the Board for International Broadcasting, the agency that oversees Radio Free Europe and Radio Liberty. He has also served on the staff of the U.S. Senate Armed Services Committee and as a senior analyst for the Northrop Corporation.

The author received a Ph.D. and M.A. from Harvard University and a B.A. from Brigham Young University. Dr. Porter is the author of *The USSR in Third World Conflicts* (Cambridge University Press, 1984) and has published numerous articles on Soviet foreign policy and U.S. national security.

Foreword

"The Army is the leading detachment of the Party!" The political upheavals of the past half-decade have forced Western students of Communist military establishments to take a critical look at this timeworn slogan. There was for many years no serious doubt that ruling Communist parties, in Europe and elsewhere, had created an extremely successful system of political control over the institutional instruments of coercion. But "civilian" domination of the military was exposed to the same pressures that affected the other institutions of Communist politics. The result, when Communist rule entered its terminal crisis, was to permit new and unexpected variations on the army's old relationship to the Party.

The pattern of civil-military relations in any one country is unique, the product of factors and forces that are not combined in the same fashion anywhere else. Yet, allowing for these variations, four broad patterns have emerged in the crisis of communism: (1) joint opposition to radical reform by both military and Party leaderships, (2) joint support for radical reform, (3) an institutional split in which the military supports reform, and (4) a split in which the army is the chief defender of the old order.

Of these four patterns, the most obvious—and by all our old assumptions about the staying power of communism, the most predictable—was military support for a determined effort by the Party to protect the power and privileges that they both enjoyed. A united front of this kind would have been consistent both with the traditional Western view of civil-military relations and with Communist parties' long-standing resistance to democratization. We have seen this pattern in certain countries—China is the outstanding example—but it has been the exception rather than the rule.

At the other extreme, a truly loyal high command might have been expected to offer support for a consistent reformist program under Communist Party leadership. Six years of *perestroika* under Mikhail S. Gorbachev convinced most Western analysts that the Soviet military would mount no full-blown challenge to reform, despite periodic grumbling over its pace and content.

These first two patterns took for granted a continuing accord between civilian and military leaderships, but in some Communist countries cooperation between these two institutions began to unravel. Facing organized popular opposition, generals often proved unwilling to risk a bloody defense of the old regime: to do so would have exposed them to personal dangers and violated the veneer of independent professionalism that many of them had sought. In Poland, the military distanced itself from the Communist Party gradually, over a period of years; there was no single moment in which the generals had to switch sides. In Romania, by contrast, the decision not to back the Ceausescu regime had to be made overnight.

The August 1991 coup in the Soviet Union also ended with senior officers showing their unwillingness to bear the stigma of repression. But this pattern emerged only after the scale of popular opposition to the coup became clear. Until then, it seemed that what might be emerging was a rare case of military readiness to wrest political control from a reformist civilian leader. In very different circumstances, the Yugoslav military has also demonstrated its willingness to assume a leading political role in order to thwart the secession of Slovenia and Croatia.

Exploring the role of armed forces in the crisis of Communist institutions around the world has been one goal of a study launched more than two years ago by the Center for Strategic and International Studies (CSIS). Under the title *Creating the Post-Communist Order,* we have sought to investigate similarities and differences within the worldwide crisis of the Communist order, the better to understand the new institutions that are being established in totalitarianism's place. We are now publishing a series of monographs that will examine the political, economic, and military dimensions of this huge transformation.

The present monograph, *Red Armies in Crisis,* is the first publication in this series. It combines high scholarship with an understanding of the needs of those who must analyze—and act upon—the events of the moment. Dr. Bruce D. Porter, who contributed to an earlier CSIS study of civil-military relations (published as *Soldiers and the Soviet State,* Princeton University Press, 1990), has made impressive order out of the disparate experiences of more than a dozen Communist states. His conclusions shed light on the crucial role of the military in one of this century's greatest political upheavals. More than this, he has helped to illuminate the upheaval itself.

CSIS is extremely grateful to the Lynde and Harry Bradley Foundation for its generous support of this project and of other work in this area.

Stephen Sestanovich
Director of Soviet and East European Studies, CSIS
September 1991

Introduction

The dramatic collapse of the August 1991 coup against Mikhail Gorbachev and the subsequent disintegration of the Soviet Communist Party followed several years of profound crisis for Communist regimes around the world. Inevitably, this crisis affected the armed forces of those regimes also. In the USSR, *glasnost* had exposed the Soviet military to unprecedented public criticism while *perestroika* had meant painful changes in military doctrine, organization, and procurement. These developments caused serious strains in civil-military relations, leading some senior military officers to join the coup attempt against Gorbachev.

Earlier, in Eastern Europe, the collapse of Communist regimes in the autumn of 1989 had confronted military officers with vexing dilemmas regarding their loyalty and mission. In China, the crushing of the student-led pro-democracy movement in Tiananmen Square by the People's Liberation Army had violated military traditions and brought to light potential divisions in the officer corps. Even in orthodox Cuba there had been signs of civil-military tension: General Arnaldo Ochoa Sánchez, a highly decorated military officer, and six associates were brought to trial in 1989 and executed for alleged drug-trafficking and "high treason."

Yugoslavia's violent descent into civil war and the collapse of the military government of Mengistu Haile-Mariam in Ethiopia in June 1991 were further symptoms of a worldwide crisis of Communist armies. It is fittingly symbolic that the self-implosion of these two regimes should have occurred in the same month as the formal dissolution of the Warsaw Pact. For it was in Warsaw, a decade ago, that the crisis of Red armies can be said to have begun with General Wojciech Jaruzelski's declaration of martial law. That action exposed the hollow shell of Communist rule in Eastern Europe, alienated Polish society from a once-revered national army, and portended many of the dilemmas now faced by socialist armies around the world.

The nature of the crisis affecting socialist armed forces varies from one country to another. There are enough common features, however, to suggest that similar underlying forces are at work throughout the Communist world. In almost every country, the prestige and standing of the armed forces underwent a marked decline beginning in the 1980s. In the USSR and Eastern Europe, public scrutiny and criticism of the military contributed to this decline; in China, a sense of public betrayal; in Cuba, perceptions of military corruption. Defense spending also declined in most socialist states, sharpening the competition of military and civilian claimants for scarce funds. Long accustomed to receiving first priority in resource allocation, military officers often responded critically to budget cuts. Civil-military tensions heightened, and rumors of military coups swept through capital cities in the Soviet Union, Czechoslovakia, China, Yugoslavia, and Poland. In many socialist countries, a variety of antimilitary phenomena emerged not normally associated with Communist rule: draft evasion, student protests, demonstrations, and other public displays of disdain toward things military.

In the Warsaw Pact countries, the Soviet commitment to *perestroika* translated into efforts at military reform. Proposals were advanced for radical changes in the size of the military, its structure, mission, training, funding, and political oversight. More debate ensued than actual reform, but some concrete steps were taken, particularly in Eastern Europe. In China, Cuba, and other Communist countries less affected by the revolution of Mikhail Gorbachev, military reform did not carry the same priority, although internal pressures for change were evident. Where military reform did occur, it is possible to discern the emergence of a "post-Communist" military order: an order or military system combining features derived from socialism with more traditional military forms of earlier historical origin.

The following pages will examine the evolution of Communist armed forces from 1986 through August 1991. The objective is threefold: to analyze the underlying forces behind the crisis of Communist armies; to understand how such armies change in crisis conditions; and to explore the nature of the post-Communist military order emerging in certain countries. The principal focus of the study is on civil-military relations. To this extent, it is largely a political analysis, concerned with classic questions of structure, process, control, and organizational conflict. The study will also delve into the broader subject of military sociology: the role of military organizations in their respective societies and the impact of society on the military. This is essential, for the crisis of socialist armies is not merely a matter of high politics or bureaucratic conflict; it is part of a larger social crisis affecting Communist systems as a whole.

Scholars of Communist military affairs have never developed a widely accepted comparative theory of civil-military relations and, until recently, have not had to address the question of post-Communist evolution at all.[1] What is now required is a completely fresh examination of how Communist militaries evolve during systemic political crises. With respect to civil-military relations, a crucial issue is the degree to which the military intervenes in politics during crises, ranging through the spectrum from passive noninvolvement to the classic "man on a white horse" scenario. As far as military sociology is concerned, our main concern is how social and political crisis affects military organizations *internally*: how those organizations evolve in conditions of systemic change.

As a roadmap for the specific case studies that follow, it may be helpful to summarize in advance the main conclusions of this study:

- Socialist armed forces are generally characterized by military professionalism and are under "objective civilian control," as defined by Samuel Huntington.[2] This professionalism is reinforced by the political controls imposed by socialist regimes, the main purpose of which is to ensure that the army remains subservient to party and state. As socialist regimes undergo crisis, or even disintegrate, military professionalism will normally preclude military coups from occurring, or at least from succeeding, and limit army involvement in politics.
- Communist armies are influenced by the same social forces affecting their country as a whole. This is particularly true of enlisted men, although officers do not live in a social vacuum either. Because of this, major shifts in public opinion are eventually reflected among military

personnel, sometimes delayed in time and mitigated by
loyalty to the regime. The general crisis of communism
in the 1980s affected the outlook and thinking of socialist
armies, preparing them in some instances to accept
transition to non-Communist rule.

- The strongest and most universal manifestation of the
  larger crisis of communism has been an upsurge in
  traditional nationalism in most socialist countries.
  Zbigniew Brzezinski has suggested that "post-Communist
  nationalism" will be a dominant force in international
  affairs during the 1990s.[3] This force will logically manifest itself in the evolution of Communist military organizations. Senior military officers tend to favor nationalism
  when it reinforces the state and to oppose it when it is
  seen as pulling the state apart, as in multinational federations. In the latter instances, the army often seeks to act
  as the unifying cement of both society and state.

- During periods of systemic crisis, the ideological indoctrination of Communist officers and soldiers usually
  proves to be less important in shaping their behavior
  than national and historical traditions, which in most
  countries predate the establishment of communism.
  When the ideological framework of the regime is under
  stress or overt attack, military organizations tend to fall
  back on these traditional values. Ideology is abandoned
  rapidly. One exception might be military organizations
  that originated directly from Communist revolutions.

- Exceptions to the general pattern of military professionalism and noninvolvement in politics are most likely to
  occur in two circumstances. The first is when the core
  values of the military are challenged by a civilian leadership bent on radical reform; in such instances, the
  military may feel it must act in its own political self-
  defense. The second circumstance is during prolonged
  political and social crises, when the military's confidence
  in the ability of civilian leaders to deal with internal
  problems is undermined. The more protracted the crisis,
  the more likely the military is to become involved politically. In such instances, military officers may view the

army as the last salvation of the state and intervene in politics accordingly.

The study that follows is divided into five parts. Chapter 1 is a discussion of the underlying causes of the crisis of socialist armed forces. The next three chapters are the heart of the study: chapter 2 concerns Eastern Europe; chapter 3, the Soviet Union; and chapter 4, the rest of the Communist world. These three chapters will review specific problems and developments in the armed forces of individual Communist countries in the late 1980s and the various ways they adapted to the changes sweeping their political systems. The historical tradition of each country's military establishment will be discussed, as well as the nature of civil-military relations under Communist rule prior to the 1980s. This will help better define what changes have occurred and the likely outlines of post-Communist military evolution. Chapter 5 is a summary of findings that will elaborate the conclusions outlined above.

1
The Crisis of Socialist Armed Forces: Underlying Causes

Throughout the 1980s, evidence mounted of a growing crisis in Communist countries around the world. The Soviet bloc countries were particularly affected. This was not merely a budgetary or economic crisis, nor a passing political or ideological struggle. The crisis of communism is a systemic phenomenon, affecting almost all spheres of life in socialist countries: economic, political, social, public health, and so on. The pervasive and cumulative nature of the problems facing socialist countries inevitably affected their armed forces as well.

The Economic Dimension

Beginning in the 1970s, a pattern of declining economic growth rates developed in almost all countries of the Warsaw Pact. The exact figures are disputed by Western economists, but almost all agree that a decline occurred. In the Soviet Union, according to Central Intelligence Agency (CIA) estimates, gross national product (GNP) growth in real terms from 1965 to 1970 averaged 5.1 percent; from 1970 to 1975, 3.0 percent; from 1975 to 1980, 2.3 percent; and from 1980 to 1985, only 1.9 percent. Official Soviet figures claim higher growth rates but also indicate a gradual decline.[1] By 1990, Soviet GNP growth had become negative for the first time in postwar history, declining in real terms about 1 percent according to official figures, 3 to 5 percent by Western estimates (some estimates put the rate of decline even higher).[2]

The economies of the USSR's allies in Eastern Europe also encountered difficulties in the 1980s. In Hungary, which had the most reform-oriented economic policy of any member of the Council for Mutual Economic Assistance (CMEA), the average net earnings of workers fell in real terms 7 out of 10 years during the decade. Negative growth occurred in 1985 and 1989, by which time Hungary was in its worst recession in more than 30 years. Czechoslovakia did somewhat better during most of the decade, achieving modest economic growth almost every year, but it, too, had entered a recession by 1990. As for Romania, it went into a virtual economic free-fall in the last half of the decade, with its GNP plummeting according to some estimates by as much as 7 percent to 8 percent in 1989 alone; food and fuel shortages imposed severe sacrifices on an already weary population.[3] Poland experienced not only negative economic growth during much of the 1980s but also severe inflation, which drastically devalued the zloty.

Declining economic growth was not the only problem facing Eastern Europe. Most of the CMEA countries faced a serious, almost intractable debt crisis in the 1980s, the result of severe balance-of-trade problems, rising energy prices, and excessive hard-currency borrowing from the West. Poland was forced to apply for rescheduling of its debt as early as 1981, and Romania followed in 1982–1983; other countries were forced to adjust their trading patterns to stave off rescheduling. The debt-to-earnings ratio of CMEA countries (the USSR and the German Democratic Republic [GDR] excluded) reached levels that made Western bankers reluctant to loan more money; this further hindered growth prospects throughout the region.[4]

Elsewhere in the Communist world, the economic outlook varied, but the general trend was downward. Yugoslavia experienced chronic economic difficulties in the 1980s and was forced to reschedule its external debt more than once. By 1989, that debt had reached $23 billion, GNP growth was negative, unemployment stood at 15 percent, and inflation at more than 300 percent. Cuba also experienced severe economic problems in the 1980s and was heavily dependent on Soviet subsidies. It was forced to ration many basic foodstuffs, even sugar, during much of the decade.[5] By 1989, its GNP growth had dropped to under 1 percent and was sure to decline further as Soviet aid dropped. In the Far East, North Korea and Vietnam both saw their growth rates decline in the latter half of the decade, with Vietnam experiencing unemployment at perhaps 10 percent and inflation at more than 300 percent.[6]

There was one prominent exception to the overall pattern of Communist economic decline: the People's Republic of

China (PRC). The average annual growth in China's gross domestic product (GDP) from 1984 to 1988 was over 11 percent, a phenomenal achievement by any standard. Such growth brought problems of its own, however, including political strains, and could not be sustained forever: in 1988, China announced austerity measures and braked the liberalizing reforms that had facilitated its growth.[7] By 1989, its growth rate had plummeted (but was still positive), and inflation had reached 27 percent. The combination of years of rapid growth with sudden deceleration doubtless contributed to the political turmoil that China experienced in 1989. The PRC nevertheless represented a departure from the pattern of long-term economic decline seen in most of the rest of the Communist world. Its crisis was less that of a system in stagnation or decline than a crisis of political and economic development.

The economic troubles that almost the entire Communist world experienced in the 1980s inevitably had an effect on military spending. Communist governments could either maintain their traditionally high levels of military spending—thus imposing further strains on their economies—or they could trim military expenditures, with the risk of inciting civil-military tensions. In the USSR, to cite one example, both approaches were tried sequentially. During the first years of Mikhail Gorbachev's tenure, military expenditures continued to grow at high rates; their overall share of government expenditures (and of GNP) may have actually increased. In 1989 and 1990, however, Soviet defense spending declined some 4 percent to 5 percent in real terms, the result of a conscious and publicly announced policy decision on the part of the senior civilian leadership.[8] This cut in defense spending was a factor in the noticeable increase in civil-military tensions that occurred after 1988.

The armed forces of almost every country in Eastern Europe also suffered major budget cuts following introduction of a new defensive doctrine for the Warsaw Pact in 1988. Poland, Czechoslovakia, and Hungary, in particular, saw large cuts in the size of their national armies. Nor was this trend confined to members of the Warsaw Pact. In 1989 the Yugoslav army claimed that defense spending had dropped from 6.17 percent of national income to 4.6 percent over 15 years and that the real pay of soldiers had dropped nearly 16 percent in one year due to inflation.[9] Even in China, despite its economic growth, the ratio of defense spending to other government expenditures dropped roughly 7 percent from 1980 to 1988.[10]

Post-Ideological Nationalism

As Marxist-Leninist ideology seemed to lose its force and even legitimacy in much of the Communist world, traditional nationalism experienced an upsurge. This was perhaps inevitable, given that ideology and nationalism have always been diametrical forces. Ideology, regardless of its philosophical basis, invariably lays claim to universal truths transcending parochial national concerns, whereas nationalism invariably exalts the particular above the universal and views claims to universal truth as potentially threatening to the nation.

This upsurge in nationalism became particularly strong in the USSR and Eastern Europe because *glasnost* made possible overt expression of nationalist feelings that had never been far from the surface. Soviet power after 1945 had forged a vast realm of civil peace—a *pax Sovietica*—stretching from Moscow to Berlin across an area of Europe that traditionally had been racked by ethnic fragmentation, nationalist strife, and unending border disputes. It was an enforced peace, but a peace nonetheless, and it temporarily removed from the European agenda many of the nationalist issues that had caused so much conflict in earlier times. Predictably, as the pax Sovietica of the postwar era began to disintegrate, the parochial nationalism and regional instability that once haunted that region resurfaced. The result was an outbreak of nationalist phenomena that had been largely suppressed or at least quiescent during four decades of Soviet domination: ethnic strife, irredentism, intraregional squabbles, mass migrations due to racial persecution, minority repression, rising anti-Semitism, nationalist rivalries, and border disputes.

It was obviously impossible to isolate the armed forces of Eastern Europe or the Soviet Union from this nationalist upsurge. Not only did it exacerbate existing ethnic tensions within armies, but it also intensified disputes between states, such as that between Hungary and Romania, which came near

to violence in 1990. Nationalism gave the armed forces of the
Soviet bloc a legitimizing basis to fill the ideological vacuum
caused by the collapse of communism. All modern military
organizations are motivated by some degree of nationalism; for
the armed forces of East European countries in particular,
nationalism provided an important element of continuity, a
sense of mission that the Warsaw Pact could no longer provide.

The nationalist upsurge affected Communist military
organizations in another way as well. Inevitably, the armed
forces were called on to contain the resulting internal strife. In
the USSR, the army became the last bulwark of the multinational federation, the main obstacle to the secessionist ambi-
tions of the Baltic and other republics. In Yugoslavia, it was the
only supranational institution that conceivably might hold
together a disintegrating polity. In Eastern Europe, armies
served as important poles of political continuity in an era of
upheaval, despite their own internal troubles. The nationalism
of the armed forces—closely linked to the nation-state itself—
acted as a counterweight to the tribal divisions within each
country, which intensified as the cement of ideology crumbled.

Political Corruption and Social Alienation

The crisis of communism in the 1980s was not caused only by
declining economic growth and a discredited ideology. It was a
systemic crisis pervading the very fabric of Communist political systems, corrupted after decades of holding absolute power
and alienated from the populations they governed. This became starkly evident during the Solidarity period in Poland
from 1980 to 1981, when the corrupt practices of government
officials became a major issue and the magnitude of the chasm
between population and state became evident to the whole
world. Poland was an extreme case, perhaps; but throughout
the Communist world this pattern held, and wherever free
expression was tolerated, even briefly, public unhappiness
with the corruption of Communist regimes came to the fore.
After decades in power, Communist regimes had simply failed
to deliver on their promises. This was evident in abysmally low
standards of living, the deterioration of public health, shortages of basic medicines, poor housing conditions, lack of

minimal hospital care, and rampant environmental pollution.
In the Soviet Union, infant mortality rates actually increased
from 1970 to 1980, while male life expectancy dropped. Even
as the military might of Communist regimes increased and
their international influence grew, their internal social fabric
began to fall apart. The result was a pervasive sense of social
alienation and public ennui in many Communist countries.

For military organizations, this social and political crisis
affected the quality of their recruits and the relationship of
senior officer corps to civilian authorities. Senior military
officers either became part of the web of corruption or they
stood apart and experienced a growing loss of respect for
civilian leaders. In the USSR, the officer corps was appalled by
the extent to which political leaders used their connections to
obtain draft exemptions for their sons during the war in Afghanistan. Internally, the Soviet military was forced to cope
with growing problems of alcoholism and drug addiction (the
latter much exacerbated by the involvement in Afghanistan),
rising crime and suicide rates among recruits, and declining
morale.

Nor were problems of corruption and social decay confined
to the Soviet military. Following the events of June 1989, the
Chinese military conducted a major crackdown on personal
corruption in its ranks (corruption and nepotism had been
issues raised by the student demonstrators of the pro-democracy movement). Fidel Castro's charge in 1989 of drug-dealing
by top Cuban military officers suggests that corruption had
permeated even a military organization renowned for its
revolutionary ardor—and this in a regime not hesitant to
punish deviation.

The social crisis and internal corruption of Communist
countries was connected with the aging of virtually every
Communist leadership in the world. Long tenure in office
seemed to coincide with corruption and stagnation. The 1980s
saw the beginning of a massive generational transition
throughout the Communist world, indicated by the length of
tenure of many Communist leaders when they finally left the
scene: Leonid Brezhnev (USSR), 19 years; Todor Zhivkov
(Bulgaria), 35 years; János Kádár (Hungary), over 30 years;
Erich Honecker (GDR), 13 years; Nicolae Ceausescu (Roma-

nia), 26 years; Gustáv Husák (Czechoslovakia), 19 years; Josif Brod Tito (Yugoslavia), 27 years; Mao Zedong (China), 27 years. A similar generational transition is pending in several other countries and will surely be consummated in the 1990s: Castro has been in office in Cuba for 32 years, Kim Il-sung in North Korea for over 40 years, and Deng Xiaoping has held paramount rule in China for 15 years. Vietnam has changed leaders more often, but the majority of its central leadership are elderly veterans of its wars with France and the United States. Crises have occurred in virtually every Communist country where a generational transition has taken place; where the transition is still pending, crisis has not occurred.

Development of New Security Paradigms

A final dimension of the crisis affecting socialist armies was the introduction of new security policies. In the Soviet Union, the advent of "new thinking" on security affairs and a more cooperative approach to relations with the West meant a major readjustment of military doctrine. In Eastern Europe, the Soviet decision to give Warsaw Pact countries free rein in both internal and external affairs led in 1989 to the decommunization of most countries and the development of wholly new security policies. Withdrawal from the Warsaw Pact became the stated objective of more than one regime, and Hungary even expressed interest in joining the North Atlantic Treaty Organization (NATO). By June 1991, the Warsaw Pact had formally disbanded. Radical changes such as these could not help but put new strains on military organizations already coping with the challenges outlined above.

The development of new security paradigms was most obvious in the countries of the former Soviet bloc, but evolution of security strategies also began to occur elsewhere, partly as a ripple effect of the changes in Soviet foreign policy. North Korea for the first time in its history began to explore the possibility of a rapprochement with South Korea. China was no doubt amazed to see the USSR fulfill the three preconditions it had set for improved relations: withdrawal from Afghanistan; reduction of forces on the Chinese border; and an end to Vietnamese occupation of Cambodia. Gorbachev's visit to

China in May 1989 and the souring of relations between China and the United States that took place following Tiananmen Square both pointed to a partial realignment in China's diplomacy. In all of these cases, the military was forced to adjust its thinking and policies accordingly.

2
Crisis and Revolution: East European Armed Forces

From August 1989, when Tadeusz Mazowiecki became the first non-Communist prime minister in the Warsaw Pact, until December 1989, when Nicolae and Elena Ceausescu were condemned to death by a military tribunal in Romania, every ruling Communist government in the Warsaw Pact either fell from power or underwent drastic political change. The following year, the German Democratic Republic disappeared from the map, incorporated into the Federal Republic by the terms of a broad European agreement settling most of the outstanding issues left from the Second World War. The East German army likewise disappeared, its remnants incorporated into the Bundeswehr. Of the remaining countries, only the Communist regime in Bulgaria clung to power after the country's first democratic election. Poland, Hungary, and Czechoslovakia elected non-Communist governments; Romania remained under more authoritarian rule, although its government also renounced communism, at least formally.

The reunification of Germany makes the case of the East German army essentially moot for our purposes. The following survey will concentrate on Czechoslovakia, Hungary, and Poland, with a briefer look at Bulgaria and Romania. It will also look at one country outside the Soviet bloc but in the same region: Yugoslavia. These countries (Bulgaria excepted) represented the only truly ex-Communist countries in the world as of mid-1991. The evolution of their armed forces since 1989 provides valuable insights into how socialist military organizations will adapt to radical changes of regime that bring with them sharp shifts in mission, ideology, and loyalty.

Czechoslovakia

Until 1968, the Czechoslovak People's Army (ČLA) was widely considered to be the best military organization in Eastern Europe. "Operating on the basis of a well-educated population, a sophisticated industrial base, and a heritage relatively free of anticommunism, the armed forces were exemplary of the new socialist armed forces, red and expert."[1] The Soviet invasion of Czechoslovakia and the "normalization" that followed were devastating to the ČLA. Between 1969 and 1975, more than 11,000 officers were purged from the armed forces, the Gottwald Military-Political Academy was closed, numerous officers were relegated to reserve status, and the reenlistment rate of junior officers plummeted. Even after normalization was declared accomplished in 1975, the ČLA remained somewhat of a black sheep among Warsaw Pact armies, often assigned to garrison responsibilities during maneuvers and surrounded by other national forces.[2]

The Czechoslovak army, unlike many of its counterparts in Eastern Europe, lacks any strong identification with Czech nationalism. Czechoslovakia gained its independence in 1918 as a result of the Treaty of Versailles, not through a war of liberation. In 1948, the new Czechoslovak Army stood aside from politics during the Communist overthrow of Eduard Beneš, and it did so again in 1968, during the Soviet invasion, when it remained confined to its barracks. This tradition of strict political neutrality and noninvolvement reflects the professionalism of the ČLA, but it also means that the army is not viewed by the Czech population as a bulwark of the state or repository of national trust.

This tradition of political neutrality and noninvolvement was very much evident during the chaotic events of the autumn of 1989. In October, as the crisis of communism in Eastern Europe became evident and police clashed with demonstrators in East Germany, General Milan Vaclavik of the Czechoslovak army, who was the minister of defense, emphasized publicly that "members of the Army fully support the Party's policy" and that the military would "responsibly implement the tasks entrusted to it by the Communist Party and the ČSSR [Czechoslovak Socialist Republic] government."[3] Two weeks later, he told a high-level gathering of military commanders that "our Army . . . actively supports the policy of the CPCZ [Communist Party of Czechoslovakia], and resolutely rejects the demagogical demands of the illegal structures."[4]

True to its tradition of noninvolvement, the ČLA took no overt measures to aid the beleaguered regime of Miloš Jakeš during the dramatic "Velvet Revolution" of November 20–25, 1989, but the supreme command did issue the following statement:

> Representatives of the Czechoslovak People's Army view with concern the events taking place in our country. We reject the anarchy being sown by external and internal antisocialist forces. We actively support the efforts of the Czechoslovak Communist Party Central Committee . . . aimed at overcoming the complex socio-political situation, at establishing calm and order.[5]

One day after this statement was issued, the Jakeš government resigned in the face of public protests involving as many as 500,000 people in the streets of Prague.

Less than two weeks later, the Defense Ministry did a complete about-face. Under a new minister of defense, General Miroslav Vacek (still a military officer, rather than a civilian as the democratic opposition group, Civic Forum, had urged), the ministry announced that all references to the leading role of the Communist Party would be removed from army documents and that Marxism-Leninism would no longer be taught in military schools. On December 19, the defense minister went a step further by issuing Order Number 28 abolishing all Communist Party organizations in all units and institutes of the army.[6] The formal decommunization of the Czechoslovak People's Army thus took about three weeks to accomplish.

The rapidity of this shift reflected not merely opportunism on the part of newly appointed military leaders but also the natural tendency of the army to fall back on its tradition of political neutrality. It illustrates that more than 40 years of political indoctrination, carried out with particular intensity from 1968 to 1975, had little permanent effect on the thinking, outlook, or loyalties of the Czechoslovak army as a whole. Beneath the surface, the army remained much the same institution it had always been. In retrospect, this is fairly obvious, but in the uncertain situation that followed the Velvet

Revolution, there were concerns among the Czechoslovak public as to what position the army would take. Twice during December 1989, the Ministry of Defense felt compelled to make public statements disavowing any plans for a military coup.[7]

Almost immediately following the November revolution, there were public demands for reform of Czechoslovakia's military service requirements. By January 1990, more than 150 army units were involved in hunger strikes and other protest activities in support of sweeping military reform. The new government and Defense Ministry quickly responded to these demands. Defense Minister Vacek had proposed in December that the term of military service be cut from 24 to 18 months (and from 12 to 9 months for university graduates) and that the number of reservists be reduced by 90,000. He also indicated that he could support some form of alternative service for conscientious objectors. By the end of January, these provisions had been passed into law by the Federal Assembly. At the proposal of Czechoslovak President Václav Havel, the name of the army was also changed to Czechoslovak Army (the word "People's" being dropped.)[8]

During the course of 1990, Havel's government continued to reform the Czechoslovak defense establishment. In view of the new service requirements, the size of the army declined drastically, from 200,000 to 140,000. By September, more than 10,000 officers and noncommissioned officers (NCOs) had been discharged from service, the majority at their own request. Czechoslovakia's defense budget was cut by 15 percent, and Havel announced that the country would develop a new doctrine and new organization for the armed forces. In October, Havel dismissed General Vacek as defense minister and replaced him with a civilian, Lubos Dobrovsky. On that occasion, Havel went out of his way to emphasize that Vacek had performed with complete loyalty and competence, but he indicated that Czechoslovakia's political development required the appointment of a civilian as defense minister.[9]

By comparison with the stormy course of military reform in the USSR, the reforms in Czechoslovakia were as "velvety" as the November revolution. There were, however, minor perturbations along the way. Some 5,000 officers resigned in 1990, many in protest over cuts in personnel and budget. A smaller minority were discharged for refusing to take the new loyalty oath that omitted reference to the Communist Party. During the year there also arose a radical reform organization within the military—the Free Legion—that lobbied for more rapid military reforms and called in September for the dismissal of Vacek. Perhaps partly to dispel the notion that Vacek's subsequent dismissal had resulted from pressure by this group, the new defense minister suspended the organization's activities within the army upon his appointment.[10] Another problem that surfaced in 1990 was the inevitable personnel issue involved in coming to terms with the Communist past. In January 1990 the Czechoslovak army command set up a commission to rehabilitate and compensate the thousands of officers who had suffered because of their activities during the Prague Spring. Conversely, demonstrations took place in Prague in March to demand the resignation of military officers who had expressed support for the Soviet invasion.[11]

Such predictable problems aside, Czechoslovakia's transition from a Communist state and army to a non-Communist order took place with remarkable ease. The almost overnight speed with which the Czechoslovak army adjusted to its new political overseers marks it as a classic professional (i.e., nonpolitical) military organization and provides a textbook example of how national tradition tends to prevail over ideology in the long run. In February 1991, when a ground offensive against Iraq was launched in the Persian Gulf, soldiers from Czechoslovakia were deployed along with U.S. and allied armies for the first time in 45 years, symbolically completing the full circle of evolution that the army had experienced since the collapse of Communist rule only 15 months earlier.[12]

Hungary

Traditionally, the military was "one of the most highly regarded classes within Hungarian society."[13] By the end of World War II, however, the Hungarian army was a shattered organization, physically decimated by the war and spiritually bankrupt as a result of its long collaboration with Nazi Germany. Its failure to prevent the Soviet takeover of Hungary did not help its reputation, nor did the subsequent Stalinist remaking of the army under Communist rule. From a nationalist perspective, perhaps the one saving grace of the Hungarian army between 1938 and 1989 was the spontaneous participation of many army units in the resistance against the Soviet invasion of Hungary in 1956. That event helped the army recapture a sense of identity with the nation, which it somehow managed to preserve despite the political uniformity imposed on it after the invasion.

From 1956 to 1989 the Hungarian army was the smallest army in the Warsaw Pact, and Hungarian defense spending was the lowest of any pact country, both in absolute and per capita terms. Hungary was a faithful member of the pact, and most senior military officers were members of the Hungarian Socialist Workers Party (HSWP), but the reform course (so-called goulash communism) charted by János Kádár enabled the Hungarian military to develop under conditions more open and tolerant of reform than those in most East European countries. In 1980, for example, Hungary reduced its mandatory military service from 24 to 18 months, and there were serious attempts under Kádár to improve living conditions and social services for the military. Hungary was also the only country in the Warsaw Pact *not* to possess a uniformed security police. These relatively liberal conditions mirrored the relative liberality of Hungarian society within the Soviet bloc.

It is difficult to choose a precise date for "the end of communism" in Hungary. If one had to be picked, though, it would probably be November 26, 1989, the date of the first free national election in 42 years. Strictly speaking, however, that election did not choose a new government but only determined when the first real presidential election would be held. The first freely elected, non-Communist government assumed power only in May 1990; its election was the culmination of years of gradual reform. Hungary became non-Communist as the result of evolution, not revolution. As a result, by 1990 the pace of change in Hungary arguably was lagging behind that of other countries of Eastern Europe. The changes that occurred in the military likewise occurred more gradually in Hungary than in Czechoslovakia or Poland.

Some effort at military reform had already begun under Károly Grosz, who had replaced Kádár in 1988. It originated in part from the Party's hope that it could retain popular support and political power by adopting a more radical reform path than that taken in the past. In August 1988, an alternative to military service was established for the first time.[14] In the fall of 1989, the authority of Party organs in the military was abolished, and Defense Minister Ferenc Karpati, in an address to an army conference in Budapest in September, emphasized that the army must remain politically neutral—a servant of the nation, not an instrument to be used against the Hungarian people. The abolition of Party control organs in the military quickly led to a marked rise in the number of military officers leaving the Party as well as a dramatic decline in the number of officers applying for membership.[15]

The period leading up to the November 1989 election was marked by uncertainty and tension, not only in Hungary but throughout Eastern Europe. Sandor Petres and Robert Ribanszki, hard-line members of the HSWP and leaders of a minority faction in the Party, spoke openly of the possibility of military intervention to save Hungarian communism from its imminent demise. In August, Petres even told the Budapest daily *Mai Nap* that his group was "prepared to seize power through a military putsch." Such claims were immediately repudiated by the army, the Defense Ministry, and the Workers' Guard.[16] The probability of direct intervention in political affairs by the Hungarian military was always low and by this time was virtually nil.

This was true despite the fact that Hungary was in the process of massively cutting back its defense expenditures. Only a month after the rumors about military intervention, the government announced budget cuts in defense spending of nearly 18 percent, with additional cuts to follow. It also proposed cutting the membership of the Workers' Militia (a volunteer reserve militia set up in 1957 to help bolster the Kádár regime) from 60,000 to 40,000.[17] When the reduced budget was presented to the National Assembly by the chief of staff of the Hungarian army, Colonel General Jozsef Pacsek, he pleaded for an end to further cuts, claiming they would destroy the army.[18]

It did not take long for additional cuts to be made. Prime Minister Miklos Nemeth announced in December that military service would be reduced from 18 months to one year and that the size of the army would be cut by the end of 1991 by an additional 20 percent to 25 percent over the cuts already announced. This would reduce the army to only 63,000 soldiers and would entail significant cuts in the officer corps. The Defense Ministry also announced a major reorganization, creating a clear division between the civilian functions of the ministry and those of the army command. What was left of the Political Directorate was completely abolished, leaving the military solely in charge of the education of its troops. These changes were all linked to Hungary's adoption of a new defensive doctrine and to the depoliticization of its army.[19] Simultaneously with the announcement of these changes, Pacsek's retirement was announced, as well as that of a handful of other senior military officers. The Defense Ministry also reported that nearly a quarter of the Hungarian general staff and about 50 colonels had resigned in protest against these cuts or the earlier cuts announced in September. This was the strongest (and really the only) outward indication of dissatisfaction in the Hungarian army over the new direction the country was taking.[20]

The most interesting developments affecting Hungary's military during 1990 were the radical changes occurring in Hungarian foreign policy. There had been talk prior to 1989 of Hungary withdrawing from the Warsaw Pact; during 1990, this became a formal goal of Hungarian foreign policy. In May 1990, Jozsef Antall became prime minister of Hungary, and the Communist Party went into formal opposition (a fate it had accepted as inevitable since the previous November). Upon formation of his cabinet, Antall announced his support for Hungary's withdrawal from the Warsaw Pact, a proposal the Free Democratic party had already introduced into Parliament. Although some viewed this as "filing for divorce from a dead wife," formal withdrawal was pursued by Hungary throughout 1990 in bilateral talks with the USSR and in various Warsaw Pact meetings.[21] In February 1991, this objective was essentially overtaken by events when Gorbachev proposed to dismantle the military structure of the pact on April 1, 1991.

If neither the Warsaw Pact nor the "threat from the West" gave the Hungarian military a justification for existence, the continuing conflict with Romania did. The end of *pax*

Sovietica in Eastern Europe had seen the revival of long-standing tensions within the region, the most prominent of which was the historical dispute between Hungary and Romania. In the last years of Ceausescu's rule, the government in Budapest had issued increasingly outraged protests to the Romanian government over the treatment of the two million Hungarians living inside Romania, most of them in Transylvania. In mid-1989, in connection with its development of a new defensive doctrine, Hungary identified Romania as its greatest security threat and transferred troops from its southeastern region to its border with Romania. By 1990, the dispute had become the main focus of Hungarian security concerns, entirely eclipsing East-West issues or even the relationship with Moscow.

By mid-1990, more than 30,000 refugees had fled Transylvania for Hungary, their swelling numbers a reminder of the plight of their ethnic counterparts across the border. In March 1990, interethnic riots in the Transylvanian city of Tirgu-Mures had left several dead and hundreds injured. The incident brought polemics between the two capitals to a new height, and there was serious talk about the possibility of a conflict. Coming only weeks before Hungary's first free parliamentary elections, the situation might have been used by either the HSWP or the military as a pretext for opposing democratic change, but this did not occur. The military, in fact, made positive efforts to reduce tensions both at home and with Romania. By October, the defense ministers from both countries had met and agreed on measures to improve cooperation and reduce the risks of confrontation. Nonetheless, Hungary's defense plan promulgated in 1990 called for the withdrawal of its troops a specified distance from all of its borders *except* the one with Romania.[22] Coinciding with the rapid dissolution of the Warsaw Pact, the Hungarian-Romanian conflict symbolized the triumph of nationalism over ideology in Eastern Europe.

Poland

The military in Poland has always enjoyed a considerable measure of public prestige and nationalist legitimacy. Prior to the declaration of martial law in December 1981, the military trailed in popularity only behind the Catholic church and the independent trade union Solidarity. Its prestige derived from such events as the achievement of Polish independence in 1918 under the leadership of wartime hero Jozef Pilsudski, the defeat of the Soviet army on the Vistula in 1920, and the impressive performance of the First and Second Polish Armies in the closing battles of World War II. Even under Communist rule, the army was regarded as more loyal to the nation than to the Communist Party or its Soviet overlords in the Warsaw Pact. The decision of the army to back Wladyslaw Gomulka in his showdown against Nikita Khrushchev in 1956 had confirmed this loyalty, and many credited the army's nationalist allegiance with having deterred the USSR from ever invading Poland despite periodic internal troubles similar to those that had triggered intervention in other East European countries.[23]

The relationship between the Polish military and society changed following the declaration of martial law in 1981. Although enforcement of martial law against civilians was undertaken largely by security forces—paramilitary forces and police (such as the hated ZOMO)—the Polish military suffered some loss of public standing as a result of its own role in suppressing the Solidarity movement. General Wojciech Jaruzelski's claims that he had acted to save Poland from the even worse fate of a Soviet invasion did not greatly affect the public's judgment on this score, particularly not after evidence mounted during the 1980s of close collaboration between the USSR and the Polish military during the months leading up to martial law.[24]

Strictly speaking, the declaration of martial law was not a military coup. The order came from General Jaruzelski, it is true; he was acting, however, not only in his military capacity but also as first secretary of the Polish United Workers Party (PUWP). His actions, moreover, had the full sanction of Moscow and of the Party. The military was not intervening against Party authorities but really on their behalf against Polish society. The fact that a military man was head of the Party was in itself an extraordinary situation, however. During the months leading up to martial law, the military had assumed many key positions in the Party and state, culminating in Jaruzelski's appointment to head the Party.

The result of martial law was to accelerate this trend. As one observer put it,

> The imposition of martial law . . . both resulted from and contributed to the dramatic ascendancy of the military over all other institutions of the system . . . in the militarization of all, or almost all, visible aspects of public life, and in the assumption of major decision-making positions by military personnel.[25]

A Military Council of National Salvation governed the country for several years, and military officers assumed numerous positions in the government that normally would have gone to civilians. Under such circumstances, the PUWP declined both organizationally and politically. It did not help much that the majority (perhaps 85 percent) of Poland's senior officers were Party members. Poland was a Communist state in name, but a military dictatorship in practice. This type of government was not entirely new to Poland: Pilsudski, too, had presided over a military dictatorship from 1926 until his death in 1935. Jaruzelski, however, did not enjoy Pilsudski's status as a hero, and he had the misfortune of representing a discredited ideology and a hated foreign power.

Military rule did little to resolve Poland's internal troubles. It did not promote economic recovery; it did not prevent Solidarity from continuing to function; and it did not in the end keep the restless Polish population from forcing the pace of political change in Poland and throughout Eastern Europe. These failures inevitably reflected on the military itself. In April 1989, Jaruzelski's government was forced to make massive concessions in the roundtable talks with the democratic opposition, which led—more rapidly than anyone had expected—to partly free elections, then to establishment of the Warsaw Pact's first non-Communist government in August 1989.

The roundtable agreement left control of the military and security forces in the hands of the PUWP. This only put the Polish army further out of step with Polish society. After August, there were unusual popular manifestations of anti-military feeling in Poland, including a number of peace rallies on city streets and at universities. Students at two universities in Lublin, for example, boycotted mandatory military training classes and demanded elimination of the training requirement. The independent press also carried reports about the poor morale and living conditions of Polish soldiers.[26]

Poland's army had already been cut by 11,000 in the first half of 1989. Under pressure from Solidarity, the student movement, and Mazowiecki's government, additional cuts of roughly 22,000 took place between September and December. Thousands of troops were demobilized, several military units were permanently disbanded, stockpiles of weaponry were retired, and it was announced that the defense budget would be cut more than the 4 percent announced the previous June. In February 1990, Poland promulgated a new defensive doctrine that downplayed Poland's role in the Warsaw Pact and no longer identified the capitalist West as the archenemy. Drafted by a committee that included representatives of the old regime and the new government, the document was greeted with some skepticism in Poland, but it does seem to have represented a turning point in the country's formal military doctrine.[27]

The depoliticization of the army had been a long-standing demand of the Solidarity movement. In November 1989, several steps in this direction took place: the Main Political Board was abolished; ideological indoctrination was replaced by emphasis on national traditions and values; and soldiers were banned from joining political parties (a dramatic change for those who were longtime Communists). Although the military remained under the command of Jaruzelski, Prime Minister Mazowiecki and other non-Communist ministers served on the National Defense Committee, giving them input into the making of the country's defense policy.[28] In July 1990, the old guard Communist general and defense minister Florian Siwicki was replaced by Rear Admiral Piotr Kolodziejczyk, and the last redoubts of Communist influence began to disappear rapidly from Poland's political affairs. The replacement of General Jaruzelski by Solidarity leader Lech Walesa as president of Poland in December 1990 completed the process. By that time, the military had made a massive retreat from participation in Poland's political life, and few military officers held posts in the government. The fact that Walesa did not even invite Jaruzelski to his inauguration reflects the decline of the army's political standing despite its several years of almost supreme rule in the 1980s.[29]

It is fascinating to note that the Polish military rapidly recaptured a measure of its nationalist legitimacy and standing after Jaruzelski's departure. Admiral Kolodziejczyk's appointment accelerated the pace of change in Poland's defense establishment (the Polish navy having suffered no taint from martial law). The army for its part resumed its traditional posture as defender of Poland. Military units were no longer deployed solely on Poland's western border but also on its eastern frontier, where new fortifications were built. Ministry of Defense officials cultivated contacts with their counterparts in NATO, and the military began to take part in traditional patriotic and even religious events it had previously shunned. Kolodziejczyk announced in January 1991 that the Ministry of Defense would be restructured into a civilian ministry. Meanwhile, ministers of religion (chaplains) returned to Polish military units—only months after Communist political officers had been removed! By the spring of 1991, opinion polls showed that the Polish army was the only institution in society actually gaining in popularity (from 58 percent support in early 1990 to 62 percent in 1991).[30]

Under criticism for the hard conditions of army life, the Defense Ministry made efforts to reform its internal administration, adding a soldier's rights spokesman to act as a watchdog on conditions in the military. In the course of the year, the holder of the office of chief military prosecutor was made an appointee of the prime minister, a step intended to "strengthen the hand of the democratically elected government at the expense of the military hierarchy."[31] The Defense Ministry announced in October that compulsory army duty would be cut to 18 months. In November, Kolodziejczyk announced that the size of the Polish army would be allowed to drop to some 250,000, an additional cut of more than 50,000 men and a reduction from 1988 of some 40 percent.[32]

Having lost a great deal of prestige and nationalist legitimacy as a result of martial law, Poland's professional officers corps appeared determined not to make the same mistake again. It not only failed to resist the dramatic changes thrust on it after August 1989, but it positively supported them. By September 1990, Poland's Defense Ministry was hosting talks with senior defense officials from Czechoslovakia and Hungary on the future of the Warsaw Pact, talks from which the USSR was deliberately excluded because, in the words of Deputy Defense Minister Bronislaw Komorowski, "democracy there has not advanced far enough."[33] By January 1991, Poland was actively preventing the transit of Soviet trucks and supplies across its territory in order to get bargaining leverage in negotiations over Soviet troop withdrawals and transit rights. As in Hungary and Czechoslovakia, national interest and traditional values triumphed rapidly over the legacy of 40 years of ideological rule.

Bulgaria and Romania

The continuity of Communist authority in Bulgaria, despite a measure of democratic reform, and the persistence of authoritarian rule in Romania have hindered the pace of military reform in these countries. Yet the course of their military affairs since 1989 manifests the same tendency to return to nationalist roots that has been noted elsewhere. In post-Zhivkov Bulgaria, for example, military officers have been emphasizing professionalism and depoliticization, seeking to regain the high public trust and prestige that the military enjoyed prior to World War II. Within the armed forces, a quasi-official organization—the Bulgarian Legion Georgi Stoikov Rakovski—has been established "to promote professionalism in the army and to campaign for soldiers' rights."[34] Named after Bulgaria's best-known nationalist and revolutionary leader of the nineteenth century, the legion was organized in May 1990. Its founders specifically identified their objective as raising the professionalism and prestige of the military.

The organizers of the legion went out of their way to emphasize that it would be politically neutral and would encourage strict obedience to commanding officers. This was an important commitment, because the Bulgarian military, unlike most of its East European counterparts, had a long tradition of active interference in politics. The army had plotted the overthrow of Prince Alexander of Battenberg in

1903 and had engineered a coup in 1934; army elements may also have attempted an abortive coup against Todor Zhivkov in 1965. The military is not known to have played a direct role in the ouster of Zhivkov in November 1989, but Colonel General Dobri Dzhurov, then minister of defense, was probably among the inner circle that pressed for Zhivkov's resignation. Given this tradition and the political uncertainty now weighing upon Bulgaria and the Balkan region in general, Bulgaria must be judged as likely a candidate as any in Eastern Europe to fall under military rule at some point in the future.

In Romania, of course, the armed forces intervened massively in politics when they threw their support to the anti-Ceausescu uprising that occurred in December 1989. What exactly happened during the critical week leading up to the Romanian dictator's overthrow remains uncertain, but it is known that large segments of the senior officer corps threw their support to the popular uprising beginning around December 21. Prior to that, military units (as well as the Securitate, the country's secret police organization) had obeyed orders to fire on the demonstrators crowding Romania's streets, resulting in the death of thousands. After December 22, the top command refused to support Ceausescu further, and many military units joined in the resistance. A senior military commander, General Ion Hortopan, broadcast a message to the country affirming the support of the army for the uprising.[35]

The military's involvement appeared at the time to be essentially spontaneous. Certainly there was no attempt to establish a military government, and in fact the military commander of the crucial Timisoara District, Major General Gheorghe Popescu, told Western correspondents within days of Ceausescu's overthrow that the army "probably" would support any government chosen by the people.[36]

This image of a quiescent army intervening only briefly in politics to support a popular uprising against a hated dictator turns out to be only part of the story. In the more than a year that has passed since the December revolution in Romania, new information has come to light about the involvement of the military in those events. Particularly interesting were the revelations of General Stefan Kostyal, former deputy director of the Romanian army's Political Directorate.[37] Kostyal, who had been dismissed from his post in 1970 for having criticized the regime, revealed that there had been a military plot to overthrow Ceausescu in 1984 that had been aborted at the eleventh hour when the regime learned that something was afoot. Kostyal also claimed that many of the same conspirators who plotted on that occasion were involved in the December 1989 revolution. Although the uprising itself was popular and spontaneous, many of the actions of senior military officers followed the outlines of the plan originally agreed on as early as 1984.

Although it is impossible to confirm Kostyal's claims independently, his account does fit the facts as they are known and has not been contradicted by other military officers involved in Ceausescu's overthrow. It also correlates well with an account of events by one of the military officers who guarded Ceausescu after his arrest. The latter account also seems to confirm rumors that the national defense minister, General Vasile Milea, who was reported to have committed suicide at the peak of the revolution, was actually executed by the resistance forces.[38] The military, in other words, did not act as a united front against Ceausescu but divided into at least two factions, the larger of which joined the popular uprising.

Under the government of Ion Iliescu, the military seems to have reverted to its more traditional passive role. There are some signs, however, of ferment beneath the surface. When the Iliescu regime decided to use force against antigovernment demonstrations in Bucharest in June 1990, it did not turn to the military but to miners brought in from outside the city, former Securitate dressed as miners and soldiers, and other nonmilitary elements that supported the government. Either the government lacked confidence in the army or the army refused to participate in the action against the demonstrators. The fact that military uniforms were worn illegitimately by some of the progovernment forces that put down the demonstration suggests that the government wanted to create the impression of military backing where it may not have existed.[39]

Sometime during 1990, reform-minded Romanian officers set up an organization known as the Action Committee for Democratization of the Army. The group was officially banned in June but continued to operate sub rosa: the Romanian press

agency Rompres reported in September that two army majors
from the group had been forced into reserve status, and in
November the group published demands for the government
and parliament to investigate the army's role in suppressing
demonstrations prior to December 22, 1989. More recently,
the organization demanded the ouster of Romania's defense
minister, General Victor Stanculescu, for his alleged role in
repression of the December revolt in Timisoara. This demand
followed the dismissal of seven officers on the executive committee of the organization from active duty in the army.[40]

This reform wing in the army is not representative of the
military as a whole but reflects the greater room available for
political action in post-Ceausescu Romania. The army's own
traditional penchant for autocracy can be seen in a communiqué issued by an army unit in Bucharest in November 1990
in the middle of a further wave of demonstrations and strikes
in Romanian cities. The communiqué condemned "destabiliz-
ing and violent" elements that were threatening the country's
independence and distorting the image of the military. The
same document also pledged, however, that the army would
remain neutral in politics. By the end of 1990, there were said
to be continuing tensions between President Iliescu and Defense Minister Stanculescu, whose replacement by a civilian
was demanded by an article in *Azi*, the daily newspaper of the
Romanian National Salvation Front.[41]

Romania remains an unstable country with an uncertain
and tenuous relationship between the military and civilian
authorities. Such a situation is not new in Romanian history
and is likely to lead to considerable tension, turnover, and
political maneuvering at the top. Between 1930 and 1940, the
post of chief of the General Staff changed nine times in Romania, and it would not be surprising if a similar instability
prevailed during the next several years.[42]

Yugoslavia

In most of Eastern Europe, the crisis of communism has led to
the collapse of Communist rule. In Yugoslavia, the crisis of
communism may lead to the collapse of Yugoslavia. After three
years of mounting crisis, Yugoslavia in the spring and summer

of 1991 descended into violent strife bordering on all-out civil war. Units of the Yugoslav National Army battled sporadically with rebel forces in Slovenia and Croatia in an effort to prevent the secession of the two republics. While political leaders on both sides of the conflict struggled to find a political solution, the top officer corps of the Yugoslav National Army, dominated by Serbian officers, announced its determination to prevent disintegration of the country. The Yugoslav crisis underscored the significance of the Yugoslav National Army as the force that originally unified the country during the partisan campaigns of World War II and as possibly the only supranational force still capable of holding it together. At the same time, it starkly dramatized the difficulty faced by a multiethnic military force in a disintegrating multinational state.

Yugoslavia was not a member of the Warsaw Pact, nor is it under the direct influence of the USSR. Its internal crisis stemmed more from internal causes than from winds of *perestroika* coming out of Moscow. The collapse of communism in Eastern Europe, however, intensified pressures for change in the Balkan country. From 1988 to 1990, the League of Communists of Yugoslavia (LCY) undertook sweeping political and economic reforms that essentially ended its monopoly on political power. Prime Minister Ante Markovic bluntly told the Extraordinary 14th Congress of the LCY in January 1990 that the federal government no longer answered to the Party and could exist without it. By May 1990, the LCY or its affiliates had lost multiparty elections in four of six republics, and Party membership had plummeted drastically.[43]

From its earliest origins, the Yugoslav army has regarded itself as the defender of Yugoslavia's Communist Party. Aside from the army itself, the LCY was the only strong supranational institution binding together the ethnically diverse country's six republics and two autonomous provinces. The officer corps of the Yugoslav army regarded the disintegration of the LCY's authority with dismay but took no direct action to forestall it. By December 1990, the army itself had been formally depoliticized by a law banning all political parties from operating within its ranks (in practical terms, this affected only the Communist Party). Without a legitimizing ideology, the Yugoslav National Army fell back on its traditional role of defending the unity and federal system of Yugoslavia. Many officers, however, joined a new political party, the Communist League-Movement for Yugoslavia, founded by former Army Chief of Staff Stefan Mirkovic.[44]

Even prior to this, rapid urbanization, skyrocketing inflation, and rising nationalist sentiment had placed great strains on Yugoslavia's federal structure. The slide toward civil war had begun as early as September 1989, when Slovenia's National Assembly promulgated 54 amendments to its constitution intended to enhance the republic's sovereignty; among other things, the amendments restricted the federal government from deploying troops in Slovenia without the consent of the republic's assembly. Two senior military officers, Colonel General Stefan Mirkovic and Vice Admiral Petar Simic, denounced the amendments as violations of the federal constitution and stated that the Yugoslav army recognized only the authority of the federal state. Simic told a Central Committee plenum of the LCY that the army "belongs to Yugoslavia," that it was "equally Croatian, Serbian, Macedonian, Slovenian, Moslem, Montenegrin, and all the nationalities in our country."[45] In subsequent party plenums, military leaders stated flatly that the armed forces would not stand by idly as the country disintegrated. The intentions and motivations of the army were viewed with much suspicion in Slovenia, if only because 70 percent of Yugoslavia's military officers were Serbs (versus a 40 percent ratio in the general population) and the army was therefore seen as a tool of Serbian domination.

The dispute between Slovenia and the federal state was not the only ethnic division threatening Yugoslavia. Kosovo had been deeply troubled for many years and became more so following attempts by Serbia early in 1989 to curtail the province's autonomy; in 1988 and 1989, tension also mounted between Macedonians and Albanians in Macedonia and between minority ethnic groups and dominant ethnic groups throughout Yugoslavia. The Slovenian secession effort, however, was the most serious mounted by any republic, and Croatia lagged only slightly behind Slovenia in its opposition to federal rule. The conflict between these two northwestern republics and Serbia, the largest republic in the country, was the one that finally plunged the country into civil conflict.

During the course of 1990, both republics took steps toward possible secession from Yugoslavia, including the establishment of republican militia forces. In turn, the Yugoslav Secretariat for National Defense on September 28 banned the republics from maintaining military units outside the national military structure. The Slovenian National Assembly responded by dismissing the commander of Slovenia's Territorial Defense Forces (an officer in the Yugoslav army) and replacing him with a Slovenian officer. On October 2, the collective State Presidency ordered forces from the Fifth Military District to reassert control over the Slovenian militia, stating that Slovenia's move imperiled the federal constitution. Two days later a small unit of Yugoslav military police seized the headquarters building of the Slovenian militia. This action did not immediately trigger violence, but it was denounced in Slovenia and caused a dramatic heightening of tension throughout Yugoslavia.

The sense of crisis deepened in December, when Croatia also assumed direct control of its territorial defense forces. Federal Defense Secretary Colonel General Vejko Kadijevic said publicly that no country in the world had several armies and warned that "Yugoslavia must not and will not become another Lebanon."[46] A few days later Croatia demanded Kadijevic's resignation, while the Slovenian National Assembly voted 203 to 0 to hold a plebiscite on independence. The State Presidency ordered Croatia to disband its new militia force. When it refused to yield, the Defense Ministry issued a warning: "If all mobilized armed units in Croatia are not disbanded immediately, the Yugoslav National Army will take action."[47]

The Yugoslav army, in fact, did not take immediate action against Croatia, but from this time until June 1991, Yugoslavia was in perpetual crisis, with the prospect of civil war looming ever closer. In mid-March, tens of thousands of anti-Communist protesters (mostly Serbs) occupied downtown Belgrade, calling for Serbian leader Slobodan Milosevic and other ministers to resign. These protests, motivated primarily by anti-Communist sentiment, weakened the central government at a critical juncture. As the crisis unfolded, the army requested that the State Presidency meet in emergency session, reportedly to impose "a military solution."[48] The State Presidency rebuffed the suggestion, leading three of its members to resign. At the peak of the crisis, top military officers disappeared from public view for a few days, fueling speculation of an impending coup. The supreme command issued a five-point statement on March 20 warning "that it would not under any circumstances allow interethnic clashes and civil war" in the country.

In April and early May, federal troops entered several villages in Croatia to protect Serbian ethnics from violence; there were reports of armed clashes with local police. In one incident, antimilitary protesters in the coastal village of Split shot and killed a soldier of the Yugoslav National Army. The military reaction was swift. Federal Defense Minister Kadijevic issued a statement widely viewed as an ultimatum to the federal government. Claiming that the country was already in a civil war, he demanded that civilian authorities declare a state of emergency and order the disbanding of all armed units not under army control. If the civilians did not act, Kadijevic said, the Yugoslav National Army would intervene. Although many Yugoslav observers believed that the military was merely bluffing, the collective State Presidency responded to Kadijevic's ultimatum by convening three days of crisis meetings. These ended with agreement on a plan for disarming paramilitary units that fell just short of declaring martial law. The State Presidency also sought to defuse ethnic tensions by appointing a commission to review disputes between Serbs and Croats.[49]

The State Presidency's peace plan proved stillborn, because Croatia and Slovenia refused to disarm their local militia. Within a week, a worse crisis erupted when the State Presidency failed to agree on a new president. By the traditional pattern of ethnic rotation, the post should have gone to a Croat, but four republics, including Serbia, voted against the Croatian candidate, Stipe Mesic, on the grounds that he wanted to break up the union and would make sure he was the last Yugoslav president. This action only added fuel to a rising fire. Again, General Kadijevic weighed in. After a meeting of top military commanders in Belgrade, he called for installation of a new state president as soon as possible and for implementation of the earlier order on disbanding paramilitary units.[50]

On May 19, Croatia held a referendum in which 94 percent of the population voted in favor of Croatian sovereignty within

a loose confederation. Eleven days later, the Croatian National
Assembly passed a resolution favoring a declaration of sovereignty and independence. The Croatian defense minister
announced that Croatia would form its own army. Slovenia
took similar steps toward independence, claiming control over
its armed forces, taxes, foreign trade, and customs levies. The
Yugoslav National Army began moving large numbers of troops
into the rebellious republics. By June, there were 20,000
troops stationed in Slovenia alone. Once again, a familiar
pattern ensued: faced with possible civil war and demands for
order from the military, Yugoslavia's political leaders attempted to compromise. Early in June, leaders from six republics reached tentative agreement on a plan to allow republican
sovereignty within a confederal structure that would retain
control of foreign affairs; individual republics could field militia
forces, but an all-Yugoslav military would remain in place.[51] In
a likewise familiar pattern, this compromise lasted only briefly,
because the State Presidency continued to deadlock over
appointing a new president to head the state.

Early in the evening of June 25, Croatia and Slovenia
crossed the Rubicon, formally declaring the independence of
their republics. The Yugoslav government immediately pro-
claimed the declarations null and void and ordered the army
to secure Slovenia's frontiers with Italy, Austria, and Hungary
and to police the border between Croatia and Slovenia. After
two days of maneuvering and minor clashes, the first serious
fighting took place on June 27, when Yugoslav National Army
troops attacked Slovenian border posts and attempted to seize
the airport in Ljubljana. Slovenia reported 100 killed or
wounded in these clashes. Again, the pattern of crisis leading
to short-lived compromise ensued. On June 30, the government in Belgrade ordered its troops to withdraw from Slovenia,
and the next day the State Presidency finally agreed to appoint
the Croatian Stipe Mesic as president. Slovenia and Croatia
agreed to suspend their declarations of independence for three
months.[52]

The cease-fire lasted two days. Humiliated by their poor
performance against the Slovenian militia, senior military
commanders hardened their political stance. After the army
high command warned Slovenia against harassing retreating

army units, fierce fighting broke out in parts of Slovenia. General Blagoje Adzic, the army chief of staff and a Serbian known to favor intervention, declared that "under the existing circumstances, a truce is no longer possible" and "full-scale combat activity" would resume. As hundreds of tanks and armored fighting vehicles rolled toward Slovenia and Croatia from bases south of Belgrade, the Yugoslav government announced that the military was acting on its own and without authority. Prime Minister Markovic reportedly said that "the army is out of control."

The large-scale clashes that occurred from July 2 to 5, when another cease-fire began, were a moment of truth for the Yugoslav armed forces, a time when their own internal strains and weaknesses came into clear focus. Although the army apparently acted on its own in renewing the offensive against Slovenia and Croatia, it made no attempt to stage a coup, and it supported political efforts to negotiate a new cease-fire. The Yugoslav military was torn between conflicting goals at the heart of its self-image: on the one hand, preserve the Yugoslav federation at any cost; on the other hand, act as a professional army, loyal and obedient to civilian authority. The dilemma was compounded by Yugoslavia's multinational structure. General Adzic admitted that hundreds of Slovenian soldiers, including entire units, had deserted during the fighting. But ethnic loyalties alone did not define the military's position. The deputy defense minister, Vice Admiral Stane Brovet, himself a Slovene, played a prominent role on the federal side throughout the hostilities. Similarly, Defense Minister Kadijevic is a Serb but a known opponent of hard-line nationalists, such as Milosevic.[53]

Humiliated by the poor combat performance of the Yugoslav National Army in Slovenia, the top military command took several remedial steps even as the crisis continued in July: thousands of Serbian reserves were called up, many mid-level officers were reassigned, and deserters were threatened with execution. Political leaders in Serbia and Croatia viewed such steps with alarm, convinced that the army was becoming a primarily Serbian force that would impose its domination on the whole country. Yugoslavia oscillated between civil strife and hastily arranged cease-fires throughout July. Numerous clashes occurred, causing hundreds of casualties. Desertions plagued the army, largely among its non-Serbian troops. Croatian and Slovenian officials claimed that about a thousand troops from each nationality had defected by mid-July. By August, it appeared that the army was gaining control of Croatia, while abiding by an earlier agreement to stay out of Slovenia. Kadijevic and other military officers continued to issue statements calling for preservation of the federation, although even the relatively hard-line General Adzic claimed that the army was committed to a peaceful solution of the crisis.

Tito's former ally-turned-dissident Milovan Djilas has accused the Yugoslav army of being nostalgic for the days of Tito. Others have suggested that the army wants to preserve the country largely for its own self-interest. The motivations and intentions of the Yugoslav officer corps are more complex than either of these explanations. Angry at civilian inaction, the army has refrained from attempting a coup. Faced with the worst ethnic strife in Yugoslav history, the multi-ethnic officer corps has remained largely intact, despite desertions at lower levels. Tempted to use force indiscriminately, it has actually shown restraint on numerous occasions (although this restraint may yet erode as the war in Croatia continues). Attempts to blame the crisis on the Communist inclinations of the officer corps also miss the mark. It appears that many officers are motivated by genuine commitment to a country that has existed as a single political unit for 46 years. They are also deeply concerned that the Yugoslav army acquit itself well as a fighting force. They are, in other words, military first, Yugoslav second, and Communist, if at all, only a distant third.

In the uncertain months that lie ahead, the survival of Yugoslavia as a state, as well as the kind of state it becomes, will hinge in large measure on the attitudes and actions of the Yugoslav National Army. A military coup appears unlikely, but the army will wield enormous political influence and may largely shape the contours of federal policy, even without rebelling openly against civilian authority. Yugoslavia's national crisis and its ultimate resolution will also offer glimpses into the challenges likely to be faced in the future by yet another multinational Communist state: the Soviet Union.

3
Crisis and Adaptation: The Soviet Armed Forces

The Brezhnev era, particularly its first decade, is regarded by many Western analysts as a golden era in Soviet civil-military relations.[1] A high degree of comity prevailed between civilian officials and senior military officers; the defense establishment consistently received a first prior claim on resources; there were few international or domestic issues on which Party and army strongly disagreed. In the later Brezhnev years, however, there were signs of civil-military discord and of mounting problems in the defense establishment. The appointment of a civilian, Dmitrii Ustinov, to replace Marshal Andrei Grechko as minister of defense in 1976 may have been viewed as a snub by the officer corps. Speeches by Brezhnev, impassioned statements on military issues by Marshal Nikolai Ogarkov (chief of the General Staff from 1979 to 1984), and high-level meetings between Brezhnev and top officers on budget priorities all suggest that resource stringency was becoming an issue between the Communist Party of the Soviet Union (CPSU) and the military. The invasion of Afghanistan in 1979 confronted the Soviet military with its first major shooting war since 1945, bringing with it the tactical and budgetary problems associated with any conflict. (There is little evidence, however, that the actual invasion was a major point of civil-military disagreement.)[2]

Only after Brezhnev's death did more serious signs appear of civil-military tensions and mounting problems in the military. The most dramatic indicator of a more troubled era was Ogarkov's sudden dismissal in September 1984 as chief of the General Staff. Although he was transferred to an important command post, this was widely viewed as a demotion. Western analysts have propounded numerous theories explaining his fall, but the evidence is too scanty to be conclusive. The marshal's abrasive personality was well known, and his dismissal may have been partly a personal matter, not reflecting larger issues. (Ogarkov's thinking on military issues, laid out in various publications both before and after his demotion, remained influential among the Soviet officer corps and may have influenced Gorbachev's reforms, as will be discussed later.)

Minor indicators of civil-military strains continued to appear in the early years of Gorbachev's tenure. Military officers were less prominent at major events at Red Square; Ustinov's immediate successors, Marshals Sergei Sokolov and Dmitrii Yazov, were both appointed candidate members rather than full members of the Politburo like their predecessors. Sokolov's dismissal as defense minister in May 1987, following the Cessna affair, clearly reflected civilian determination to hold the military accountable for its errors; whether this was the sole reason for his dismissal must remain a matter of speculation. The fact that his successor, Yazov, was not in the first tier of the Soviet officer corps and was already associated with moderate reform positions suggests Gorbachev wanted changes in the Soviet military.

None of these early events, however, can be interpreted fairly as reflecting a crisis in Soviet civil-military relations. Shortly after entering office, Gorbachev had intensified the war in Afghanistan, and the share of total government expenditures devoted to defense appears to have increased slightly. It was only in 1988 that changes in Soviet foreign policy, the effects of *glasnost,* and Gorbachev's reform policies began to affect the Soviet military seriously. From around the time of the 19th Party Conference in 1988, the pace of change in Soviet foreign and defense policy stepped up, and signs of internal military turmoil and civil-military conflict burst into the open. In April 1988, shortly before the conference, *Pravda* published a hard-hitting critique of corruption and poor discipline in the military that could only be seen as a signal of civilian intent to reform the armed forces.[3] One instrument to accomplish this was *glasnost* itself. By 1989, the Soviet press was publishing highly critical articles on the armed forces, unprecedented in their tone and frankness. Western observers spoke of the Soviet military as being under siege, and issues of military reform, control, structure, and even procurement began to be debated openly. The senior officer corps responded defensively, and signs of serious demoralization surfaced in the rank and file.

The analysis that follows will focus on the period from the 19th Party Conference until the attempted palace coup of August 1991. It will examine five main issues: (1) conditions of military life, particularly the hazing of recruits; (2) draft evasion; (3) the debate over resource allocation; (4) the security policy of the Soviet Union; and (5) the impact of nationalism and republican separatism on the military. These five sections will be followed by an analysis of the failed coup. A concluding section will consider prospects for serious military reform and the likely future of civil-military relations in the USSR.

Conditions of Military Life

The abysmally poor conditions of life in the Soviet military have received considerable publicity in the *glasnost* era. Soviet conscripts enter an army troubled by numerous social ills, among them crime and substance abuse, and one where the hazing and physical abuse of conscripts are endemic. The quality of housing, health care, hygiene, and nourishment in the armed forces is seriously lacking, far below even relatively low Soviet standards. One report even attributed a high rate of desertion from Soviet Air Defense forces (reportedly 60 deserters a month) to the miserable living conditions and hardships of military life.[4] Such shortcomings have led to demands both from the public and from within the military for improvement of the safety, well-being, and living standards of Soviet troops.

The problem has been greatly compounded by the pending return of thousands of Soviet troops from Eastern Europe to the USSR, where there is insufficient housing to accommodate them. Colonel General Boris Gromov, former commander of Soviet troops in Afghanistan, told reporters in August 1990 that the military supported the withdrawal from Eastern Europe but that "the immediate problem now is the guarantee of proper living conditions for our officers and NCOs." Military officers concerned about the problem formed a special association, *Shchit* (Shield), to lobby for better living conditions for servicemen; its membership by the end of 1990 was reported to be as high as 200,000.[5]

Social Ills

Other social ills troubling the Soviet army read like the pathology of a terminal patient: alcoholism, drug addiction, crime, corruption, suicide, psychiatric disorders. It was perhaps inevitable that the same ills facing Soviet society would be found in the military, given that "virtually all social, regional, ethnic, and cultural groups are represented in the intake of new conscripts."[6] Because the social problems facing the military originate from the larger crisis of Soviet society and have been linked with the need for military reform, it may be useful to review them briefly:

Rising crime rates. Military Prosecutor Aleksandr Katushev told the press agency Novosti in September 1990 that the crime rate in the Soviet armed forces had increased by 40 percent in the previous six months. He claimed that serious crimes had risen more than 20 percent, assault with intent to injure by more than 40 percent, and rape by nearly 16 percent. In defense of the military, he claimed that the civilian crime rate exceeded that of the military.[7]

Suicide. In June 1990, Major Vladimir Lopatin, a people's deputy and outspoken advocate of military reform, claimed that 45 percent of Soviet conscripts suffered from psychological disorders and that thousands of Soviet soldiers die each year, 20 percent of them by suicide. He later reported that as many as 800 Soviet soldiers commit suicide annually. In December 1990, Defense Minister Yazov cited an only slightly lower figure of 500 suicide deaths during the preceding year.[8]

Alcoholism. The problem of alcoholism is acute in Soviet society, and the military has not been exempt. Western sources estimated in 1988 that as many as 25 percent to 30 percent of the soldiers serving in the Group of Soviet Forces in East Germany were full-fledged alcoholics.[9] Soviet soldiers in Eastern Europe have often left their bases without permission to buy or steal alcohol, and they have often attempted to drink substitutes, such as brake fluid or perfume. The problem is not new, however, nor is it confined to Eastern Europe. In 1990 *Krasnaia zvezda* reported that 22 soldiers in the Kamchatka Peninsula had been hospitalized after drinking antifreeze![10]

Physical Abuse and Hazing

The social ills outlined above, serious though they are, have not received nearly as much publicity as another problem of more immediate concern to conscripts and their families: the physical abuse and hazing of Soviet enlisted men by other soldiers or officers. The informal system of hazing, known as *dedovshchina* or *starikovstvo*, had existed in the Soviet military for years but had rarely been discussed openly until the era of *glasnost*. (A Soviet army defector, Viktor Suvorov, describes the practice vividly in a work published in the West in 1984.)[11] The subject was raised at the 20th All-Union Komsomol Congress in 1987, prompting a rash of reports on the problem in the Soviet military press, most of which minimized the problem. One delegate to the congress, however, published a short story on the subject, *"Sto dnei do prikaza"* (One hundred days until the order), in the popular journal *Yunost'*, which caused an upsurge in public concern. Soviet newspapers and magazines were flooded with letters on the subject; *Komsomolskoe znamia* declared that no other single work on the army had prompted as much reaction.[12]

The debate and publicity have raged ever since. From mid-1988 to mid-1991, at least 100 articles appeared on the subject in major Soviet publications; this was in addition to dozens of letters, television reports, and publicity in smaller publications or in the unofficial press. A survey indicated that only 40 percent of conscripts were aware of the problem in the 1970s, but by 1990 virtually 100 percent were aware (as were 90 percent of their parents).[13] More than half of these articles appeared in the military publication *Krasnaia zvezda*, which hardly suggests the military was trying to sweep the issue under the carpet. In fact, a division of opinion was evident in military publications, with many officers, apparently veterans or more senior officers, disputing the extent or severity of the practice and other younger or more reform-minded officers confirming that the problem was serious.

The *dedovshchina* problem was exacerbated by ethnic tensions in the armed forces. When draft evasion and desertion among Baltic recruits rose dramatically in 1989, many reports attributed this to prejudice against Baltic soldiers, who were often subject to beatings, rape, and other abuses by Russian and Central Asian soldiers. The mysterious deaths of numerous soldiers from non-Russian republics further incensed public opinion on the subject and prompted demands that soldiers be allowed to serve in ethnically homogenous units in their own republics. Defense Minister Yazov acknowledged that the problem of hazing had been exacerbated by nationalist tensions but refused to countenance the formation of ethnic units.[14] In May 1990, *Argumenty i fakty* reported that 80 percent of all criminal hazing incidents in one unit were ethnically based, a figure that had risen dramatically in one year.[15]

The massive publicity given to *dedovshchina* evidently helped sensitize military officers and prosecutors to the problem. The deputy chief military prosecutor, Major General Valerian Parfyonov, reported in October 1989 that the number of criminal incidents of hazing had declined 20 percent from the first half of 1988 to the first half of 1989.[16] He attributed this to more stringent efforts at controlling the practice by the General Staff and Military Prosecutor's Office. He acknowledged that the problem remained serious and that in recent months it had taken on increasingly ethnic dimensions. He even claimed that in 1989 there had not been a single criminal case registered of violence between soldiers of the same nationality, aside from a few cases of assault between Russians.

Despite this apparent improvement, the image of the military was further tarnished in 1990 by a report that some 15,000 Soviet soldiers had died over the past four to five years as a result of physical abuse, suicide, or negligence.[17] By this time, rising public concern had compelled Gorbachev to issue a presidential decree establishing a special commission to investigate peacetime deaths or injuries of Soviet servicemen.[18] The publicity *glasnost* gave to the social ills of the military, and especially to *dedovshchina,* unquestionably damaged the reputation of the armed forces. This appears to be a sore point between the top military leadership and its civilian counterparts. Yazov commented in December 1988 on the effect of negative publicity on the armed forces: "Everyone must understand that this is a question of great political significance, a question of the army's prestige and of the faith that the Soviet people have in it." Several months later, Yazov claimed that media reports had caused "the spread of discrimination against officers, direct moral and physical insults against them and the development of unhealthy circumstances around military bases." Figures released by Soviet defense officials substantiated Yazov's claim, indicating that 85 Soviet officers had perished in 1989 as a result of civilian attacks, nearly half of them deliberate murders.[19]

Draft Evasion

Draft evasion first surfaced as a significant problem during the war in Afghanistan. Senior military officers were troubled by the efforts of some civilian elites to seek draft exemptions for their sons. Several articles criticizing the practice appeared in the military and civilian press. These early reports of draft evasion did not necessarily reflect a rift between military and civilian authorities. It is significant that articles in *Krasnaia zvezda* on draft evasion criticized the behavior only of local *government* (not Party) officials in regions of the country far removed from Moscow.[20] In any event, civilian and military authorities soon found themselves in accord on the issue, because the problem of draft evasion did not diminish but increased after the Soviet withdrawal from Afghanistan in February 1989.

Antimilitary protests took place at numerous higher institutes of education in the Soviet Union in the course of 1988, even after it became clear that withdrawal from Afghanistan was imminent.[21] That same year, the government announced that the mandatory military service of most university students would be deferred until after their studies. This was a return to the policy in effect prior to 1982, when service deferrals had been sharply curtailed due to the war in Afghanistan. There were signs that the military opposed the deferrals, but not nearly so vehemently as they opposed the next shift in conscription policy. In July 1989, the Supreme Soviet passed a decree ordering the *deactivation* of more than 176,000 students on active duty in the Soviet armed forces. This step elicited vociferous protests from the military, including Yazov himself, who lobbied against it during his confirmation hearings before the Supreme Soviet.[22] The defense minister com-

plained to *Komsomolskaia pravda* that the discharge of
students had caused a "difficult situation." He objected vigorously to the notion of extending draft deferments to technical
students, observing that "we have nobody to draft into the
Army—we're facing our fourth successive demographic decline." This was one of the first disputes to erupt openly
between Gorbachev's government and the Soviet military—
and the military lost decisively. (As late as the summer of
1991, the Ministry of Defense was still seeking to eliminate
student draft deferments, proposing legislation to the Supreme
Soviet that would vitiate the reform of two years earlier.)[23]

The discharge of students may have encouraged further
draft evasion, because the problem increased significantly in
1990. In June, the General Staff released figures showing that
two months into the conscription period the percentage of
draftees reporting for service was only 33 percent in Georgia,
19 percent in Lithuania, 13 percent in Latvia, and 8 percent in
Estonia, while in Armenia no drafters presented themselves at
all. The figure for the entire country was 26 percent. Some
Western news accounts mistakenly reported these as final
draft figures, causing exaggerated predictions of Soviet military
collapse in the West. But by any measure, the figures were low.
The picture was confused further when the deputy chief of the
General Staff in charge of manpower issues told TASS in July
that the spring draft had turned out a success, after all.[24]
Shortly thereafter, *Krasnaia zvezda* published figures compar-
ing the percentage of draft fulfillment in the spring of 1990
with the previous year (see table 1). These figures are prob-
lematic and must be regarded with caution. The figure for
Georgia, for example, is lower than had been reported in June.
It also seems improbable that Azerbaijan would fulfill 100
percent of its obligation and Armenia only 7.5 percent. But
even if the figures are only partly accurate, they do show an
increase in draft evasion, especially in the Baltic states and the
Caucasus. Western journalists linked the rise in draft evasion
in the Baltic region to the violent abuses committed against
recruits from those republics by Russian soldiers enraged by
Baltic demands for independence.[25]

In 1990 and 1991, Soviet reports painted a confusing
picture of the draft situation. Deputy Chief of the General Staff

Table 1
Draft Fulfillment in the Soviet Republics, Spring Call-ups,
1989 and 1990
(percentages)

Republic	1989	1990
Azerbaijan	97.8	100.0
Moldavia	100.0	100.0
Ukraine	97.6	99.4
Kazakhstan	100.0	99.2
Byelorussia	100.0	98.9
RSFSR*	100.0	98.6
Tadjikistan	100.0	92.7
Turkmenistan	100.0	90.2
Kirghizia	100.0	89.5
Uzbekistan	100.0	87.4
Latvia	90.7	54.2
Estonia	79.5	40.2
Lithuania	91.6	33.6
Georgia	94.0	27.5
Armenia	100.0	7.5

Source: *Krasnaia zvezda,* July 12, 1990.

* Russian Soviet Federative Socialist Republic

Grigorii Krivosheev told TASS in September 1990 that draft
evasion had increased sixfold over the 1988 figure. Krivosheev's gloomy report was contradicted, however, only a few
days later by his superior, Chief of the General Staff Mikhail
Moiseev, who informed the *Washington Post* that the spring
draft had been more successful than the fall draft of 1989!
Moiseev denied that draft evasion was a serious problem,
claiming that only 2,500 conscripts had failed to appear,
compared to 6,600 the previous fall.[26] His optimistic appraisal
was intended for a Western audience and may have deliberately obfuscated an embarrassing situation, for the Soviet
press carried reports of massive draft evasion throughout the
fall of 1990. General Dmitrii Grinkevich of the Soviet ground
forces told Interfax, an independent Soviet press agency, that
some 400,000 conscripts had failed to appear for the fall draft,

while *Krasnaia zvezda* claimed draft evasion had increased 85 percent from 1989 to 1990. In October, Novosti reported on the draft in Moldavia, claiming that of 14,000 potential conscripts, 5,000 had refused to serve and 4,000 had insisted they would serve only in Moldavia.[27] These figures exceeded Moiseev's estimate for the entire country.

In April 1991, Krivosheev released official figures on the fall draft of 1990, with percentages of fulfillment broken down by republics: Azerbaijan, 84; Moldavia, 96; Ukraine, 95.1; Kazakhstan, 100; Byelorussia, 90.4; RSFSR, 95.4; Tadjikistan, 93.4; Turkmenistan, 96.1; Kirghizia, 100; Uzbekistan, 85.6; Latvia, 39.5; Estonia, 35.9; Lithuania, 25.1; Georgia, 18.5; Armenia, 22.5. These figures confirmed an overall decline from the spring draft (see table 1), particularly in the Slavic republics. The high fulfillment figure for Moldavia, however, is dubious, as it completely contradicts all other accounts.[28]

The contradictory figures cited in these reports make it impossible to quantify the precise extent of draft evasion. But there seems little doubt, Moiseev's denials aside, that the problem increased dramatically beginning in 1990. Lieutenant General Nikolai Boiko, head of the Political Administration of the Air Defense Forces, in an address to the Party Conference of the RSFSR openly criticized the government for failing to enforce conscription.[29] His speech indicated the depth of concern over this issue in the officer corps. Subsequent events suggest that those concerns were registered forcefully and effectually with the civilian leadership. Early in 1991, the Kremlin initiated what appeared to be a systematic crackdown on draft evaders. Soviet troops in Moldavia began methodically rounding up young men who had failed to report for duty, and in the Baltic states Soviet troops entered Vilnius and Riga with the purported claim of dealing with draft evasion.[30] That much larger issues were at stake was, of course, by then obvious to the whole world.

The Debate over Resource Allocation

The problems of draft evasion and the internal social ills afflicting the Soviet military have been issues on which the interests of military and civilian authorities have largely coincided. No such harmony of interest prevails, however, in an area of great sensitivity to the military: resource allocation. As noted earlier, there were signs of moderate civil-military tension over defense expenditures during the late Brezhnev years and the interregnum presided over by Yuri Andropov and then Konstantin Chernenko. Soviet defense spending continued to grow in real terms during these years, however, and the share of total government expenditures going to the military may have actually increased. Soviet Premier Nikolai Ryzhkov stated, for example, that the original 12th Five-Year Plan (1986–1990) called for 4 percent per annum real growth in military outlays, which would have necessitated a substantial increase in the percentage of total spending devoted to the military. The first real decline occurred only in 1989, when there were real cuts in the level of Soviet defense spending for the first time in decades.

One sign of high-level military concern over planned cuts in spending may have been the resignation of Marshal Sergei Akhromeev as chief of the General Staff in December 1988. Akhromeev's resignation was made public in Moscow on the same day that Gorbachev was at the United Nations announcing a unilateral reduction of 500,000 Soviet soldiers over two years. The ostensible cause of his resignation was poor health, but the marshal's opposition to unilateral troop cuts was well known.[31] By late 1988, he also would surely have known of the cuts in weapons procurement planned for 1989. The fact that Akhromeev continued after his resignation to serve as a full-time adviser to Gorbachev suggests that his health may not have been so bad after all. Perhaps Gorbachev retained him in order to mollify military critics of the cuts and to keep open a channel to recalcitrant members of the officer corps.

Within less than a year of Akhromeev's resignation, military opposition to spending cuts had surfaced openly. Defense Minister Yazov in September 1989 told *Izvestia* that "it is economically groundless and politically short-sighted . . . to try to make reduction of defense expenditures the sole means to liquidate the budget deficit and resolve all of today's social problems."[32] He argued that savings from cuts in procurement

should be offset by higher spending on qualitative improve-
ments and by expenditures on housing and amenities for
Soviet recruits. The theme of quality versus quantity was also
raised by Moiseev:

> [The USSR] cannot permit any reduction of the armaments
> and personnel of the army and navy that would entail a
> lessening of their military potential, that would create an
> imbalance in military and strategic parity. From this comes
> the emphasis on the budget: we cannot fall behind the
> leading states and their armies in the development of
> military science and research and design work.[33]

Early in 1990, the military publication *Kommunist
vooruzhennykh sil* carried a roundtable discussion with
Akhromeev, Yazov, Moiseev, Deputy Minister of Defense for
Armaments Vitalii Shabanov, and the chairman of the Supreme Soviet subcommittee on defense industries, M. I.
Simonov. Every panelist except Yazov expressed concern over
the pace and direction of cuts in the Soviet defense budget.[34]
A subsequent issue of the same journal carried an analytical
article that divided up the defense budget by category and
sought to justify increases in every category.[35]

The debate over military expenditures was also joined in
the Supreme Soviet, where a special commission reviewed
military spending and legislators made speeches in various
sessions either calling for greater cuts or insisting that the
military should not bear the brunt of fixing the Soviet
economy. The military was not accustomed to having its
priorities debated in parliamentary commissions. The deputy
chairman of the RSFSR Council of Ministers, Grigorii
Yavlinsky, told the RSFSR Supreme Soviet that the Defense
Ministry refused to provide budget information to working
groups of the RSFSR parliament, yielding only after Gorbachev
intervened personally.[36]

In May 1989, Gorbachev told the Congress of People's
Deputies that the 1989 Soviet military budget was 77.3 billion
rubles, a much higher figure than previously claimed. Then, in
June, the Soviet Ministry of Defense released the most detailed
breakdown of the military budget ever offered, dividing Gorbachev's figure of 77.3 billion rubles into several categories:

Weapons procurement	32.6 billion
Research and development	15.3 billion
Maintenance of army and fleet	20.2 billion
Military construction	4.6 billion
Pensions	2.3 billion
Other expenditures	2.3 billion

Subsequently, similar breakdowns were offered for the 1990 and 1991 budgets, with total military spending put at 70.976 billion rubles in 1990 and at 63.9 billion (in 1990 prices) for 1991.[37] Although these figures appear closer to reality than the absurdly low budget figures of the past, Western analysts have serious doubts about their veracity, believing they cover only about half of actual Soviet military spending. The implication that Soviet defense spending has dropped 10 percent in real terms in both 1989 and 1990 is also disputed by most Western analysts. U.S. intelligence estimates, for example, put the degree of decline close to 4 percent to 5 percent, and some sources are even more conservative. Some Soviet publications have also questioned the credibility of the figures released by the Defense Ministry.[38] Whatever the actual figures, real cuts have taken place, sowing unhappiness in the senior officer corps. Understandably, the military has seized on the U.S. victory in the Persian Gulf War as proof that higher defense spending is needed. The Soviet military press has devoted extensive space to analysis of that conflict, emphasizing the importance of high technology weaponry. All this places Gorbachev and his political allies in a difficult political situation. Improvement in the consumer economy requires further cuts in military spending, yet these are opposed by the military, whose loyalty must be assured. The dilemma is illustrated by the problems that have arisen over the leadership's announced intention to convert hundreds of military enterprises to civilian production. The official plan calls for conversion of 550 large-scale enterprises, making possible an increase in production of consumer goods of some 270 billion rubles over five years.[39] In fact, there seems to be little serious movement in this direction, although whether because of military resistance, bureaucratic inertia, or lack of resolve is unclear. *Komsomolskaia pravda* reported in November 1990 that only five or six enterprises had been converted, while the U.S. Department of Defense reported that only minor facilities, and not a single major defense plant, had been converted to civilian production.[40] Without transferring assets from the military to the civilian sector, however, Gorbachev's government cannot realize the "peace dividend" it keeps promising.

The Security Policy of the Soviet Union

The civil-military debate did not remain confined to rubles and kopeks or even purely military issues for long. Inevitably the debate came to encompass the foreign and security policy of the USSR. Several prominent officers became outspoken critics of the "new thinking" in Soviet foreign policy: Colonel General Boris Gromov, former commander of Soviet forces in Afghanistan; Colonel General Igor Rodionov, head of the General Staff Academy and also a veteran of the war in Afghanistan; Colonel General Nikolai Shlyaga, first deputy chief of the Main Political Administration (MPA); Lieutenant General Nikolai Boiko, head of the Main Political Administration of the Air Defense Forces; Major General Leonid Ivashov, head of the Defense Ministry Affairs Administration; and Army General Albert Makashov, commander of the Volga-Urals Military District. Gromov, for example, published an article in the spring of 1990 that portrayed the security outlook for the USSR in stark terms. Gromov did not attack the civilian leadership directly, but he criticized calls for cuts in military spending.[41] In later articles, Gromov also attacked the liberal media, thereby triggering somewhat of a shouting match between himself and *Komsomolskaia pravda*.[42]

Among the issues that most frustrated the conservative critics of Gorbachev's government was the Soviet decision to allow Eastern Europe to go its own way in the fall of 1989. As the revolutionary events of that autumn unfolded, the senior military leadership initially gave every sign of supporting the hands-off policy of the Kremlin. Akhromeev professed to the Italian newspaper *La Repubblica* that the events in Eastern Europe were quite normal and that he was calm about what was happening, even if it led to a non-Communist Eastern Europe.[43] Early commentaries in *Krasnaia zvezda* also supported the new approach, claiming that the independence of Eastern Europe would "pave the way for the stability of democratic and progressive forces."[44] It was not long, however, before the question of who lost Eastern Europe surfaced. The very top Soviet military leaders, such as Moiseev and Akhromeev, voiced their concerns over the loss of Eastern Europe privately, but officers only slightly less junior to them were not so hesitant.

The most outspoken critic of the policy was Makashov. In June 1990, at the founding congress of the Russian Communist Party in Moscow he accused the top Soviet leadership of abandoning all the geostrategic gains made since World War II. "The Communists of the Army and Navy are indignant at the inaction of the Central Committee, the Politburo, and the government," he stated.[45] His remarks triggered an acrimonious debate in the days leading up to the 28th Congress of the CPSU in July 1990. *Izvestia* called for his resignation; Gorbachev defended government policies in an interview carried on Central Television; and Foreign Minister Eduard Shevardnadze defended the direction of Soviet foreign policy in a long interview carried in *Pravda*.[46]

Aside from some heckling of liberal spokesmen at the Party congress, the issue was largely confined to the working group on international affairs, where another political officer, Major General Ivan Mikulin, blamed the withdrawal of Soviet forces from Eastern Europe on the "new thinking" in foreign policy, and Admiral Gennadii Khvatov, commander of the Pacific Fleet, charged that the Soviet Union had retreated to its weak strategic position of the late 1930s, with no allies in either the East or the West.[47] Moiseev and Yazov made an insipid defense of government policies. The final document was an elegant compromise between the "new thinking" and more conservative stances that avoided specific mention of the changes in Eastern Europe. Whatever compromise may have been reached, however, did not prevent Major General Leonid Ivashov, only a few weeks after the congress, from publicly criticizing the Soviet political leadership for the withdrawal from Eastern Europe.[48]

The critical statements of Makashov and other hard-line military critics of the government are startling enough. They appear mild, however, compared with statements made by certain popular writers on military affairs who reflect the almost neo-Fascist brand of Russian nationalism characteristic of reactionary circles in the Soviet Union today. The most prominent of these spokesmen are Karem Rash, a high school teacher and publicist known to have ties with the General Staff; Aleksandr Prokhanov, a conservative novelist who for more than a decade has been seen as a co-opted advocate for the military; and Major General Viktor Filatov, editor of *Voenno-istoricheskii zhurnal,* the official historical publication of the Ministry of Defense. Filatov, a notorious anti-Semite, is credited with increasing circulation of the once-staid journal tenfold (to 277,000) by carrying highly nationalistic articles catering to reactionary elements in the military.[49]

Prokhanov early in 1990 wrote a lengthy article in the Russian nationalist publication *Literaturnaia Rossiia* that accused the Gorbachev leadership of undermining three main pillars of the Soviet system—socialist ideology, central political control, and central planning—while simultaneously dismantling the geopolitical structure of Eastern Europe. Prokhanov portrayed a bleak picture of a Soviet Union falling apart, sinking into civil war, and being dismembered by Western intervention.[50]

Karem Rash has published articles in Filatov's journal that glorify the army as the foundation of Russian society, blame Soviet ills on Western and "feminine" influences, and denounce the "new thinking." Rash portrays *perestroika* as "a regrouping of our forces before a decisive and prolonged offensive" and comes out openly for military intervention in politics: "Who recently saved Poland from national chaos, anarchy, and humiliation...the Polish army!"[51]

Extreme Russian nationalist positions such as these do not necessarily reflect the thinking of the Soviet high command, but they do find some support in the Supreme Soviet, particularly in the hard-line Soyuz faction. Among the members of that faction are two military officers, Colonel Nikolai Petrushenko and Colonel Viktor Alksnis, apparently the "boys in colonel's epaulets" whom Shevardnadze denounced in his December 1990 resignation speech.[52] These two military deputies reflect what appear to be increasing linkages between the reactionary, nationalist right and more traditional, "Old Guard" forces in both the Party and the military.

The Impact of Nationalism and Separatism in the Republics

The percentage of Russians in the senior Soviet officer corps is much higher than their percentage in the USSR as a whole, and the military leadership has been deeply troubled by demands for sovereignty in the republics, proposals for ethnically homogeneous units, and suggestions that draftees be allowed to serve exclusively in their own republic. These issues had smoldered for years and burst into prominence during 1990 as a result of increasing restlessness in the Baltic states, the Caucasus, and Moldavia. In January 1990, Soviet troops entered Baku with the ostensible mission of quelling an anti-Armenian pogrom that had broken out; although this does appear to have been their main mission, the troops also helped suppress the Azerbaijani Popular Front, which had taken a radical turn toward openly secessionist policies. Militia units from the Ministry of Internal Affairs (MVD) had previously gone into action on several occasions to put down communal strife in the republics, but the Baku mission appears to have been the first instance of regular army units engaging in combat against nationalist forces in the republics.

The prospect of conflict between the Soviet armed forces and armed militias in the republics loomed larger as the year progressed. On March 11, Lithuania declared its independence, dramatically increasing the level of tension in the Baltic states. Soviet troops shortly thereafter made a show of force in the streets of Vilnius and also helped enforce an economic blockade of the republic that forced it to suspend its declaration of independence temporarily. Draft evasion in Lithuania had soared after the March declaration, however, and in July, the republic declared its intent to conscript all 19-year-old Lithuanians into an independent national defense force that would replace Soviet military service.[53] Defense Minister Yazov responded with a letter to Lithuanian President Vytautas Landsbergis stating that the action would have a "negative impact on Lithuania's future."[54]

Although the drama in Lithuania received the most attention as the year unfolded, the Ukrainian Supreme Soviet in late July also voted to establish a Ukrainian national army, and the Moldavian Supreme Soviet followed suit in September. Colonel General Krivosheev responded to the Ukrainian decision by declaring that the defense of the Soviet Union "cannot be divided up into nationalist, republican-led compartments."[55] The Ukrainian Supreme Soviet showed no signs of changing its mind, however, and a few days later drafted a declaration recalling all Ukrainian soldiers from regions of ethnic conflict in other republics. The Lvov oblast disbanded its local draft board.

These actions probably had little real effect on Ukrainians already serving in the army. Nevertheless, they were anathema to the Soviet high command. Within less than a week, the Defense Ministry responded through an official spokesman that the USSR must maintain "a socialist, multinational, extraterritorial, and professional army." The Ukrainian parliament, evidently under considerable pressure from Moscow, moderated its declaration in October, stating that Ukrainians could serve in ethnically troubled areas with permission of the republic but still insisting that soldiers now serving in such areas return home before December.[56] Gorbachev by now evidently understood the gravity of the situation in the republics, for in mid-August he spoke before a gathering of military officers about "our *mutual* responsibility" in keeping nationalist strife from pushing the Soviet state "to the brink of disaster." He stated that "radical measures" would be necessary for regulating intranational relations.[57]

Probably in an attempt to dramatize the seriousness of the situation in the republics, General Moiseev told Western journalists in September that Moscow had quietly withdrawn nuclear warheads from areas of ethnic unrest in order to ensure their security. This was later denied by the Defense Ministry, which suggests great sensitivity on the point in the Soviet leadership and the possibility that Moiseev's comments were intended largely as a reminder to civilian authorities of the high stakes involved in preserving the federation.[58]

In mid-October, yet another republic joined the list of those officially challenging the authority of the military: the

Armenian Supreme Soviet passed a resolution suspending the All-Union law on compulsory military service. From this time forward the sequence of events leading to the military crackdown in Lithuania in January 1991 strongly suggests that top Soviet military leaders were pressing for concrete action to preserve what they saw as a crumbling federation. Draft evasion by individuals was one thing; formal repudiation of Soviet conscription laws by the republics was quite another.

On November 13, Gorbachev addressed an assembly of more than 1,000 elected military officials (people's deputies) in Moscow. He received such an unpleasant reception that it must have come to him as a rude shock. His speech on military reform, in which he portrayed himself as a defender of the army's interest, was interrupted by shouting and heckling. Military officers stationed in the republics portrayed a bleak picture of the hostile situation they faced and demanded greater support from the center in their struggle against antimilitary forces. Other speakers denounced draft evasion and desertion in the republics, the poor living conditions in the military, and the antimilitary stance of the liberal media.[59]

Even prior to this meeting, there were signs that Gorbachev sensed he needed to mollify the armed forces. In October, he had rejected liberal pleas for a limited celebration of the October Revolution and instead had issued a decree ordering military parades throughout the country. But the November 13 meeting seems to have marked a watershed. Four days later, Colonel Alksnis publicly stated in the Supreme Soviet that Gorbachev had 30 days to mend his ways or be removed from office. Although Alksnis is an extremist who clearly did not speak for the General Staff, his statement reflected mounting tensions and portended the anti-Gorbachev coup that occurred only nine months later. On November 25, the Soviet president held a press conference at which he denounced anti-Union forces, stating that he would use his recently acquired powers to defend the federation and that attempts to break it up could result in bloodshed. This was followed two days later by a television broadcast in which Yazov also denounced nationalist movements, making particular mention of the troubles in the Baltic states. It was unthinkable, he said, that the Soviet Union have anything but a "unified army."[60]

Gorbachev and top military leaders were evidently out-raged by the latest development in Latvia, where the republic's Supreme Council had called on municipalities to stop the flow of supplies and services to Soviet bases. Gorbachev and Akhromeev reportedly demanded of Latvian officials that the provision be repealed.[61] The Latvian decree may have been the catalyst for two events on November 27. That day Gorbachev issued a presidential decree protecting the rights of service-men in non-Russian republics, and that evening Yazov went on Soviet television with a terse announcement that the armed forces had been ordered to use force, if necessary, to protect military installations and personnel in areas racked by ethnic strife.[62] In retrospect, these events seem to indicate that the top leadership, both civilian and military, had agreed on the necessity of defending the Soviet federation by force. They were followed by official media efforts to stress popular sup-port for the army's position and by an announcement that Gorbachev had given military personnel the legal right to fire on civilians in self-defense.[63]

Events in December and January suggest that Gorbachev was under great pressure from the military and security forces to take a more hard-line approach. On December 1, Gorbachev issued a decree declaring null and void any laws passed by the republics that threatened Soviet defense capabilities or at-tempted to form separate armies. The next day he appointed KGB Major General Boris Pugo, a known hard-liner, and Colonel General Boris Gromov as minister and first deputy minister, respectively, of the Ministry of Internal Affairs. The unusual appointments can only be seen as evidence that the Soviet president had decided to crack down, either in alliance with or under pressure from the conservative wing of the military and KGB. (Pugo, of course, was later a key figure in the August 1991 coup against Gorbachev.) One day after these appointments, several army divisions were transferred to operational command of the Interior Ministry, a move that may explain the unprecedented assignment of a top military officer to head the ministry. On December 11, the chairman of the KGB went on national television, much as Yazov had earlier done, to criticize separatist movements and affirm that the KGB would act in defense of Soviet security. Four days

later, Gorbachev made a speech describing Soviet armed
forces as the bulwark of the state. Yegor Ligachev, a former
Politburo member who had frequently clashed with
Gorbachev, told Radio Moscow he was pleased with the
president's new stance on law and order.[64]

These events put in perspective the surprise resignation of
Shevardnadze on December 20, 1990. Criticizing "boys in
colonel's epaulets," Shevardnadze stated that "a dictatorship is
approaching . . . I cannot reconcile myself with what is happening in my country and to the trials which await our
people." In view of subsequent developments, Shevardnadze's
remarks suggest that he may have caught wind of plans for the
military crackdown that took place in Moldavia and the Baltic
states in January. Only one day after his resignation, an extraordinary congress of Soviet armed forces stationed in the
Baltic military district was held in Riga. The congress appealed
for the introduction of presidential rule throughout the Baltic
region, while demanding protection of "soldier's rights and
human dignity." The day this congress ended, the Defense
Ministry announced that Soviet soldiers in specific regions
would be permitted to carry personal weapons in their own
defense.[65]

Although many details remain uncertain, this sequence of
events leaves little doubt that the actions later taken by Soviet
troops in those republics had the approval of the highest
civilian and military authorities of the Soviet Union. The fact
that General Valentin Varennikov, commander of Soviet
ground forces, was sent to Lithuania to head up the operation
strongly indicates that it originated from the highest levels of
the government. Gorbachev probably did not give any specific
order to fire against civilians in Vilnius on the night of January
14, 1991, but clearly he had reached a decision to use force, if
necessary, to prevent further deterioration of the situation in
the Baltic republics.

This action, moreover, was not the end of coercive measures by Gorbachev's government. On January 25, 1991, the
Kremlin announced that Soviet army troops would be deployed
on the streets of major cities in joint armored patrols with
Internal Ministry militia. For the first time ever in peacetime,
the Soviet army would assume an internal police function.

Just two weeks later, Boris Pugo, the new minister of the interior, was promoted to the rank of colonel general after only two months in office, an obvious reward for service well performed. On February 6, the Soviet government announced a 50 percent increase in the number of joint army-police patrols in Soviet cities, from 1,740 to 2,636 patrols, involving over 12,000 troops.[66] And although some Soviet troops were withdrawn from Vilnius, additional units were moved into Moldavia in March, evidently in connection with the referendum on the Union. Yazov, Moiseev, Akhromeev, and other military spokesmen meanwhile continued to make strong assertions of support for preserving the Soviet federation with a single national army.[67]

By the late winter of 1990-1991, the USSR seemed to be following a path similar to Poland in 1981, with its supreme commander, Gorbachev, playing a role similar to that of General Jaruzelski. Gorbachev was a civilian, and he stopped short of declaring martial law, but the analogy was otherwise compelling. Gorbachev's acquisition of special emergency powers (strikingly similar to those the Polish *Sejm* gave Jaruzelski in 1981), his subsequent evocation of certain of those powers, and his support for military action in the Baltic states were highly reminiscent of the Polish pattern. The Soviet leadership appeared to be considering a retreat to its last bastion of safety: military dictatorship. These actions undoubtedly pleased hard-line forces in the military, the Interior Ministry, and the KGB. Their satisfaction, however, was short-lived.

By the following summer, the prospect of military rule had already receded, in part due to the strongly negative public and international reaction to the crackdown in the Baltic states. The growing militarization of Soviet politics had seriously strained the USSR's relations with the West while only serving to aggravate its internal crisis. Despite the presence of regular army troops in Moscow and the deployment of some 50,000 militia from the MVD in the vicinity of Red Square, the Soviet government proved helpless to prevent a mass demonstration in support of Russian president Boris Yeltsin on March 28. This event, coupled with mounting concerns over a two-month-long strike by miners in Siberia, seems to have prompted Gorbachev and his inner circle to retreat from military confrontation and seek a compromise. On April 23, Gorbachev and the presidents of nine Soviet republics (excluding the Caucasus and the Baltic states) signed an accord promising the transfer of significant political power and economic assets to the republics and the implementation of further democratic reforms. This accord apparently signaled Gorbachev's realization that coercive measures were unlikely to succeed, while enabling him to reclaim the now-tattered mantle of reformer.

The Military and the Palace Coup of August 1991

The nine-plus-one accord and the rapprochement that followed between Gorbachev and Yeltsin caused open consternation among hard-line Party figures and some senior military officers. Prior to this, they had reason to believe that the Soviet president had accepted their views on the necessity of an authoritarian approach to the internal situation. The hard-line Soyuz faction of the Supreme Soviet became outspoken in its opposition to Gorbachev throughout the spring and summer, with Colonels Petrushenko and Alksnis again calling for his replacement by a new leader. Marshal Akhromeev made a bitter attack on Yeltsin, Lopatin, and other liberal reformers in an interview with *Molodaia gvardiia* in June 1991. Then, on June 17, the national security triumvirate of Yazov, Pugo, and Vladimir Kryuchkov, chairman of the KGB, made closed speeches (later leaked to the press) before the Supreme Soviet in which they painted the situation in the country in the darkest of terms. This was the same session at which Prime Minister Valentin Pavlov made a surprise appeal to the Supreme Soviet for additional powers, a move apparently supported by both the military and the security chiefs.[68]

After an impassioned speech before the Supreme Soviet a few days later, Gorbachev easily turned back this challenge to his leadership by a vote of 264 to 24. The lopsided margin should have indicated to the hard-line group just how unpopular their position was, even among the Communist Party functionaries who dominated the legislative body. It appears, however, that the failure of this "parliamentary coup" only reinforced the determination of Pavlov, Yazov, Kryuchkov, and Pugo to force a change in the direction of Soviet politics. It is probable that their planning for a more serious coup dated from this event. One indication of support for their general political position came in mid-July, when Generals Gromov and Varennikov, along with 10 other hard-line Communist leaders (largely from the Soyuz faction), signed a letter in *Sovetskaia Rossiia* that claimed "the Motherland is dying" and appealed for an end to "humiliation" and "fratricidal war." The article implied that the military was the only force that could save the country from disaster. Of the signers of this letter, Varennikov is known to have been among the supporters of the August 19 coup, and there were likely others as well.[69]

In August, there were other signs of discontent on the right, particularly in connection with the scheduled signing of the Union treaty on August 20. Pavlov held a press conference on August 13 warning that a power vacuum would ensue following the signing of the treaty. A coalition of orthodox Russian Communists, ultranationalist literary figures (including Prokhanov), and some hard-line military officers announced that they would hold a founding congress of a new organization in September intended to "replace the present state power."[70] This group in fact probably had little or nothing to do with the August 19 coup, but such rumblings of reaction may have led former Gorbachev adviser Aleksandr Yakovlev to warn of an impending right-wing coup on August 16, when he resigned from the Communist Party.[71] His warning was not taken very seriously either in the West or in Moscow, perhaps partly because there had been many rumors of possible coups during the preceding year.[72] Whether Yakovlev had actual information pointing to a coup or only surmised its possibility on the basis of the growing discontentment expressed by hard-liners is not known.

The coup of August 19 and the 72 hours that followed were a watershed in Soviet history, with implications going far beyond the scope of this study. Strictly speaking, the detention of Gorbachev while on vacation in the Crimea and the assumption of power by an eight-person State Committee for the State of Emergency was not a military coup. It was a classic if poorly executed palace coup, undertaken by a coalition of reactionary leaders from several state institutions, including the KGB, the Interior Ministry, and the Council of Ministers. The number of military officers actually involved in plotting the coup appears to have been very small, which may partly account for the piecemeal fashion in which troops were deployed and the lack of adequate command and control throughout the armed forces during the 72 hours of the coup attempt.[73]

Dmitrii Yazov was among the eight-man committee that engineered the coup, but his role remains unclear as of this writing. Although the Western media generally assumed that Vice President Gennadii Yanayev, who replaced Gorbachev as acting president, was head of the coup, a little-noticed TASS bulletin of August 19 identified Yazov as chairman of the State Committee for the State of Emergency. Other evidence pointing to the prominence of his role is the fact that he visited Gorbachev in the Crimea only hours before the coup occurred. This may have been a last effort to persuade Gorbachev not to sign the Union treaty and to revert to a more hard-line approach. Later, when Yazov failed to appear at the press conference of August 19 called by the Emergency Committee and when rumors spread that he had left the Committee, some observers speculated that he had gone to the Crimea to negotiate with Gorbachev or warn him of what was taking place. This seems unlikely, however, given that Yazov was arrested and replaced by Chief of Staff General Mikhail Moiseev almost immediately after the coup began to unravel.

Moiseev himself was on vacation when the coup occurred, suggesting that he was not informed in advance of Yazov's intentions. Few generals apparently were, and this fact alone may have contributed to the rapid failure of the coup attempt. General Varennikov, commander of Soviet ground forces, was among the group that presented Gorbachev with an ultimatum to resign, but other than Yazov, he is the only general officer known to have been an active plotter in the coup. (Other names may surface as investigations continue.) Perhaps Yazov assumed that senior military officers would fall into line without question when his name appeared on the roster of the Emergency Committee. This did not happen, of course. Lieutenant General Konstantin Kobets, chairman of the RSFSR Defense Committee, rallied to Yeltsin's side within hours after

the coup began. On August 20, Interfax reported that two
senior commanders of the airborne forces had defected to the
opposition, or at least refused to carry out orders: Airborne
Forces Commander General Pavel Grachev and Deputy Commander General Aleksandr Lebed'. Grachev apparently was
arrested for his action. Colonel General Evgenii I. Shaposhnikov, commander of the Soviet air force, also refused to take
orders from the Emergency Committee. General Viktor
Samsonov, commander of the Leningrad Military District,
within hours of the coup declared a state of emergency in
Leningrad and imposed a curfew; 24 hours later, however, he
was reported to be rejecting orders from the Emergency Committee. Senior commanders were not the only soldiers to join
the opposition. Several tank units deployed in the Moscow
area also defected, announcing their loyalty to Yeltsin, as did
some elements from the Ryazan airborne division and the
Sevastopol infantry regiments.

    The coup ended too quickly to estimate how the large
majority of the senior officer corps would have reacted had its
success appeared likely. Many mid-level officers, and of course
conscripts, are known to be strong supporters of Yeltsin and
other reform figures, both in and out of the military. Nor is it
clear what role the Main Political Administration played during
the coup. Colonel General Aleksandr Ovchinnikov, first deputy
chief of the MPA, went on Radio Moscow on August 20 to deny
reports of military defections, suggesting the MPA viewed any
kind of insubordination with alarm, regardless of the legitimacy of the civilian body then claiming to exercise authority.
Likewise, we can only speculate about what took place in the
Soviet navy during the coup. Several warships deployed to the
Sevastopol area at the time of the coup, accounting for
Gorbachev's statement that he was "isolated by sea and by
land." On the other hand, it is possible that Yazov passed
down orders for the ships to deploy without revealing to any
naval commander the actual purpose of the deployment.
Gorbachev at his press conference upon his return to Moscow
said "it turned out that the navy would not participate in this
[the coup], and we were told they would not participate."

    In a curious way, two sometimes countervailing tenden-
cies—the professionalism of the military and its susceptibility

to societal trends—may have actually reinforced the reluctance of senior officers to accept orders from the Emergency Committee. Gorbachev had long been regarded as the legitimate civilian leader of the country and commander in chief; the military hesitated to acquiesce in his overthrow or to recognize another civilian body not perceived as legitimate. Seventy years of indoctrinating the military against political intervention paid off in ways the original architects of civilian control never would have imagined. The growing support in Soviet society for Yeltsin and the democratic movement also had an impact on the military's behavior, particularly at levels below the senior officer corps.

In the immediate aftermath of the coup, the top leadership of the Soviet armed forces was replaced. Moiseev acted only one day as defense minister before being replaced by Shaposhnikov, the latter being rewarded for his loyalty to Gorbachev during the coup attempt. Shaposhnikov's first act upon becoming defense minister was to resign from the Communist Party. He also announced his intention to replace 80 percent of top command personnel with new officers, although this was later clarified to refer only to the Defense Ministry Collegium, a body that includes all first deputy and deputy defense ministers (some 15 men in all).[74] Although Moiseev was not apparently implicated in the coup, his actions during the three days had cast suspicion on his loyalty. He was replaced as chief of the General Staff by General Vladimir Lobov, a mercurial figure associated with hard-line positions in the past but with a more moderate stance in recent years. Lieutenant General Grachev, who had briefly been arrested for defying the coup leaders, became first deputy minister of defense.

The arrests of Yazov and Varennikov following the coup (and there will doubtless be more arrests to follow) reduces the likelihood of a military coup in the USSR in the near future. The most likely candidates for leading such a coup are either under arrest or fleeing for political cover. (The suicide of Gorbachev's personal military adviser and former chief of the General Staff, Marshal Akhromeev, is one indication of how deeply the failed coup demoralized the Brezhnevite generation of top officers, even those not known to have been involved directly.) The coup attempt raises a host of new questions regarding the future of Soviet civil-military relations. Organizational reform, far-reaching political and command shake-ups, possibly a new system of civilian control are all likely to follow. To get some sense of the issues at stake, it may be helpful to look at the debate on military reform in the USSR that was taking place in the months prior to the coup.

Three Reform Paths for the Future

Even before the abortive coup of August 1991, turmoil in the Soviet armed forces and political system had generated calls for military reform from all points of the political spectrum. In the aftermath of the coup attempt, new calls for reform are being heard, and the issue of restructuring the military and its political controls has taken on greater urgency. There are in the USSR today at least three prominent schools of military reform, each representing competing visions of the future of the armed forces. These schools correspond roughly with conservative, centrist, and liberal political positions. Although the outcome of the August coup obviously favors more liberal reforms than would otherwise have been the case, all of these tendencies will continue to have their adherents in the months ahead. The new Soviet defense minister, General Shaposhnikov, is believed to be a forward-thinking officer who favors introducing market competition in the defense industry, but it would be inaccurate to associate him with the liberal reform school. The final shape of military reform in the USSR is likely to be a synthesis of all three schools of thought. What kind of army the USSR has in the year 2000 or 2010 will depend much on the nature of that synthesis.

The Conservative Reform School

The first school might be called the conservative reform school or even the Ogarkov school. Although Ogarkov's personal prominence and power faded after his removal in 1984, his thinking continued to exert great influence on the senior officer corps. As chief of the General Staff (1977–1984), Ogarkov had called for radical restructuring of the Soviet armed forces to enable them to compete qualitatively with the West. The word *perestroika,* in fact, may have been first used in a political context by Ogarkov in 1981, when he called for restructuring of "the entire economy, [as well as] political, social, scientific, and other institutions" to lay the foundation for enhanced Soviet military strength.[75] Although the specific outlines of Ogarkov's proposals remain vague and controversial even among his supporters, the basic notion that military restructuring is needed finds broad support among the Soviet officer corps. The top military leadership, many of whom Gorbachev appointed, seemed to understand that internal reforms are essential if the USSR is to compete with the West over the long run. For them, however, the main objective of reform is to strengthen the armed forces.[76] This school strongly supported Gorbachev's implementation of emergency measures to maintain internal order. Significantly, Ogarkov himself emerged in November 1990 to proclaim his support for Gorbachev's actions.[77]

Yazov and Moiseev clearly belonged to the conservative reform camp. Both men acknowledged the need for reform while always placing it in the context of the long-term strength and cohesion of the Soviet armed forces. They opposed changes in the conscription system or major cuts in expenditures.[78] Boris Gromov was another prominent advocate of the conservative reform school. Although critical of excessive spending cuts and of some of the specific policies pursued by the central leadership, Gromov acknowledged that Soviet troop strength should "correspond with the country's economic potential." At the same time, he made clear that his mission was to help restructure the army into a highly modern force, and he opposed depoliticizing the army by eliminating Communist Party cells or the parallel command structure of the Main Political Administration.[79]

Army General Vladimir Lobov is yet another spokesman for conservative reform. Once viewed as a candidate for chief of the General Staff, the hard-line general's star dimmed when he vigorously opposed unilateral force cuts in Europe in 1988. Subsequently appointed first deputy chief of the General Staff under Moiseev, Lobov in 1990 came out in support of a number of reforms aimed at restructuring the army and the defense industry. Although not advocating an all-volunteer military, he did suggest that there be greater use of volunteers and that the conscription system needed overhauling. Lobov's appointment as chief of the General Staff following the August anti-reform coup suggests that the conservative reform camp will continue to have a voice at the highest levels of the defense establishment.

Other prominent advocates of conservative reform include the military critics of the withdrawal from Eastern Europe mentioned earlier (Mikulin, Ivashov, Makashov, Admiral Khvatov) and Colonel General Nikolai Shlyaga, appointed head of the Main Political Administration in July 1990 at the 28th Party Congress. Shlyaga has said that the goal of reforms must be to make the Soviet armed forces "stronger, more reliable, and more modern," which captures the essence of the conservative reform position.[80] (As of this writing, there is an unconfirmed report that Shlyaga has been removed from his post.) Defense Minister Evgenii Shaposhnikov has been associated in the past with the conservative reform school. He has called for technological modernization of the air force and for market competition in the defense industry.

The conservative reform platform became a matter of public record on January 15, 1991, when the military press carried some details of reform proposals from the General Staff that were intended for submission to the Supreme Soviet. The General Staff plan included some adjustments in conscription, greater allowance for service in one's own republic, and plans for restructuring the armed forces in general. The formation of militias in the republics was ruled out.[81] That these proposals—conservative in the main, but with bows in the direction of real reform—were issued almost simultaneously with the military crackdown in Lithuania was probably coincidental, but it symbolizes the determination of the top officer corps not to allow reform to undermine the political cohesion of the USSR.

The Liberal Reform School

At the opposite end of the reform spectrum lies what might be called the liberal reform movement or even the Lopatin school, after Major Vladimir Lopatin, the Supreme Soviet deputy who is the best-known military advocate of radical reform. This school finds its greatest support among liberal politicians, such as Boris Yeltsin, and among liberal intellectuals and journalists, such as Vitalii Korotich and Viktor Altaev. It has also

attracted several uniformed officers, including (besides Lopatin) General Dmitrii Volkogonov, a Supreme Soviet deputy;
Colonels Vasilii Erokhin, Vladimir Smirnov, and Vilen
Martirosian of the Congress of People's Deputies; Colonel
Aleksandr Tsalko, a prominent military critic; and various
military officers of the parliamentary *Shchit* (Shield) faction.
The liberal reform camp has advocated the abolition of conscription, drastic cuts in military spending, and the elimination of Party cells and other political control structures in the
military.

Lopatin, who left the Communist Party early in 1990,
argued vigorously for the depoliticization of the Soviet army.
He contended that the armed forces are split along generational and ideological lines and that the Main Political Administration (of which he is an officer) is an impediment to the
establishment of a truly professional army. Lopatin attempted
to forge some ties with Yeltsin and Yeltsin's reform-minded
allies in the Russian Supreme Soviet, but he had few close
supporters in the top officer corps. According to Colonel Smirnov, Lopatin and the reform wing of the army were snubbed by
Yazov and derided by most of their fellow officers. Lopatin's
revelations about the social ills of the Soviet military have had,
however, a considerable impact on public thinking.[82]   The
impetus given to radical reform by the failure of the August
coup may breathe new life into the liberal reform school, and
Lopatin's views may be taken more seriously in the future.

The Centrist Reform Path

The third military reform camp is essentially centrist and
coincides with the general policies of the Soviet government
itself. Until the August 1991 coup, it might have been called
the Gorbachev school. The Soviet president and his allies have
occupied a precarious, highly fluid middle position between
the conservative and liberal reform camps. On the one hand,
Gorbachev clearly wants the Soviet military to remain a world-
class fighting force; he seems to recognize that this will require
high expenditures for the indefinite future and seems prepared
to back the professional military's judgment on how to accomplish the internal restructuring that both he and they agree is
needed. At the same time, he clearly would like the military to

claim a somewhat smaller overall share of national resources
to free up funds for other pressing needs. Gorbachev and his
allies have been attracted to some of the reform proposals
advocated by the Lopatin school (such as an all-volunteer
military), but in practice they have mostly paid lip service to
reform. Gorbachev, in other words, has firmly taken the
middle road, sometimes advocating reform, later retreating in
the face of military opposition. This closely resembles the
pattern he has displayed in other spheres of Soviet life as well.

The political leadership's indecision on military reform was
reflected in two prominent issues during 1990: the question of
whether the USSR should move toward a U.S.-style all-volunteer army, and the issue of political control of the armed
forces. In August 1990, Gorbachev gave a speech to military
graduates in Moscow in which he called for military reform
and tighter control of military expenditures. But on the issue
of conscription he struck a carefully crafted middle position,
simply outlining the views of the high command as well as
mentioning the alternative of an all-volunteer force. Yet there
are signs that the top Soviet leadership, both political and
military, has not totally ruled out the concept of an all-volunteer army and may even have it under consideration. In May
1991, for example, the navy began an experiment staffing
selected units on an all-volunteer basis, a step approved by the
USSR Supreme Soviet.[83]

About two weeks after his August 1990 reform speech,
Gorbachev issued a presidential decree restructuring the
political controls of the army and security forces. The decree
called for ending Communist Party control of the Main Political Administration but did not abolish Communist Party cells
within the military.[84] At the 28th Party Congress, Gorbachev
rejected depoliticization of the armed forces, a position advocated by Boris Yeltsin. In June 1991, Gorbachev issued a
decree establishing military councils in the armed forces,
"permanent collegial bodies of military-political leadership,"
which would include military commanders, MPA officers, and
in some cases local civilian authorities. The main thrust of this
decree was not to depoliticize the military so much as to make
it more accountable to the Soviet state, as opposed to the
Party, a step that mirrors Gorbachev's reorganization of Soviet

political structures in other spheres. As late as July 1991, however, Gorbachev was vigorously opposing a decree by Yeltsin seeking to abolish Communist organizations within the military on Russian territory.[85]

This example of Gorbachev's advocating "military reform" while still leaning toward a somewhat conservative position has been typical of his style. In the aftermath of the August 1991 coup attempt, the suspension of Communist Party activities makes the issue of Party cells in the military somewhat moot, of course. It will be fascinating to see if Gorbachev's collegial councils replace Party cells as a new kind of political control mechanism. If so, they will probably seek to ensure the professionalism and obedience to civilian authorities of the armed forces, without, however, the trappings and ideological baggage of Marxism-Leninism.

Toward a Post-Communist Order

The evolution of the Soviet system toward a state-dominated polity, rather than a Communist system, is rapidly taking place. The USSR, the Russian Federation, or whatever is left of the existing system in 10 years may not be a full-fledged liberal democracy, nor is it likely to resemble the form and style of governance we know today as communism. Rising nationalism and popular reform sentiment suggest that the Soviet (and/or Russian) military will evolve in a direction similar to what we have seen in Eastern Europe in the past two years.

For the present, the military will remain a forceful advocate for its own interests while confining its political role within certain broad parameters. Those parameters will be defined by its sense of professionalism and loyalty to the state, as well as by the intensity and duration of the USSR's internal crisis. As Communist ideology disintegrates, the core values of the Soviet military will remain intact, particularly those values that predate the Bolshevik revolution: a determination to maintain high levels of military spending; an aversion to political liberalism; a residual xenophobia; and a strong commitment to preservation of the Soviet federation, the traditional Russian empire. The military will strive to act as a unifying and stabilizing force, a counterweight to the centrifugal momentum of nationalism. Whether an army whose officer corps is dominated by one ethnic group can serve as the cement of a multinational federation remains to be seen. Yugoslavia's descent into civil war suggests that a multi-ethnic army is at best a very fragile bond for political unity.

As the USSR jettisons Marxism-Leninism as its political rationale, the Soviet military may fall back on legitimizing traditions from an earlier era. During 1989 and 1990, there was a notable increase in the number of articles in the Soviet military press devoted to czarist military traditions.[86] These included not only chauvinistic pieces by Russian nationalist writers such as Karem Rash and Aleksandr Prokhanov, but also more conservative articles in military publications such as *Sovetskii voin, Voenno-istoricheskii zhurnal,* and *Voennyi vestnik.* A sign of support for this trend among the top military leadership was the announcement in October 1990 that the Soviet army was planning to redesign its uniform (by 1995) to resemble the uniform worn by the czarist army.[87] A modern-ized, nuclear-equipped czarist army marching under the Russian tricolor flag may seem the ultimate oxymoron, but this seems to be where the Soviet (or at least Russian) military is headed. Its historical traditions and innate nationalism are rapidly triumphing over seven decades of ideological indoctrination.

4
Crisis and Reaction:
Socialist Armies Outside Europe

Outside of Europe, Communist countries are also undergoing internal strains and crises. The tendency in China, Vietnam, North Korea, and Cuba thus far has been to respond to internal pressures for change with repression and political reaction. Given the pace of economic development in China at least, it is doubtful such an approach can go on for long, but for now it is still too early to speak of a post-Communist order emerging in these countries. Since 1990, however, Marxist-Leninist regimes in Nicaragua, Angola, and Ethiopia have been replaced by non-Communist or coalition governments. The changes in these countries underscore the fragility of Communist rule in the Third World, particularly in cases where military rather than Party leadership dominates the system.

The People's Republic of China

The pro-democracy movement in the People's Republic of China (PRC) blossomed at the same time that *glasnost* and *perestroika* were sweeping through the USSR and Eastern Europe. It is thus tempting to link the two sets of events. The dramatic transformations occurring in the Soviet bloc did affect the intelligentsia and student movement of China, as shown by the massive student demonstrations that took place in connection with Gorbachev's May 15, 1989 visit to China. There is also no doubt that the PRC suffered from some of the same systemic problems affecting communism elsewhere— official corruption, a generational transition, nepotism, waning ideological fervor.[1] But, in at least one sense, China's crisis of 1989 differed radically from that of the USSR and Eastern Europe: it followed a period of rapid economic growth. China's crisis was not that of a system confronting stagnation and decline but a classic crisis of uneven and uncoordinated development.

This difference is crucial, because it meant that the government of China had little incentive to undertake sweeping reforms following a decade in which its system had produced impressive results. It also meant that the Chinese Party and government had claim to a greater measure of nationalist legitimacy than their counterparts in Communist Europe: they were developing China without it again becoming a vassal of the Western world. Years of economic growth made it more difficult for the military to challenge the overall political strategy of the Party, even though senior military officers were unhappy with the level of defense expenditures. Nor, in the wake of the crackdown, did China's leaders see an urgent need for systemic reforms. This became very clear in elder statesman Deng Xiaoping's important speech to the commanders of the troops in Beijing on June 9, shortly following the clearing of Tiananmen Square, in which he reviewed in detail the basic political and economic strategies of the regime and strongly reaffirmed their validity.[2]

The events of June 1989, in short, do not appear to be the signs of a system in terminal crisis but rather those of a system responding defensively to powerful social forces unleashed by its own developmental impetus. In such circumstances, one also might expect the Chinese military to act conservatively and to be skeptical of the more radical demands of those calling for change, whether in the pro-democracy movement or in the Communist Party of China (CPC) itself. To understand better the role of China's army in the Tiananmen Square crisis, it may be helpful to briefly review its role in internal Chinese politics prior to 1989.

Party, State, and the People's Liberation Army Before 1989

The close identification of the People's Liberation Army (PLA) with the Communist revolution that toppled the Kuomintang in 1949 has made civil-military relations in China quite different from those in the USSR and Eastern Europe, where revolutionary parties or outside armies enforced a new loyalty on the standing armies they inherited from non-Communist regimes. The PLA by contrast was loyal from the beginning because it was an integral part of that beginning:

The blurring of civil and military realms is clearly a reflection both of the guerrilla-based military ethic of the Chinese armed forces . . . and of the fact that the Party and the army grew simultaneously during the revolution and drew from the same cadre of leaders, with the result that Party and army leaders were frequently interchangeable between 1927 and 1952-1954.[3]

As a result, the PLA was controlled primarily through remunerative and symbolic tools rather than by means of extensive organizational checks. Frictions between the PLA and the civilian leadership of the CPC have usually manifested themselves in the form of factional struggles within the Party in which the fundamental loyalty and compliance of the armed forces is not at issue.[4]

The PLA yielded local administration to civilian authorities in 1954, and since that time it has generally refrained from direct interference in Chinese politics. The few exceptions have come about during periods of profound political crisis. Even in such instances, its involvement has generally taken place at the initiative of senior political leaders or factions within the political leadership. The most extreme example of military intervention in Chinese politics came during and shortly after the Great Cultural Revolution, when the PLA from 1963 to 1971 assumed increasingly vast powers of civilian administration, becoming in fact "the supreme political and administrative authority in the provinces and . . . a central force in Peking politics."[5] The PLA at one point controlled the position of first secretary in 21 of 29 Party committees and held 62 percent of provincial Party secretariats.

This massive military intervention in politics originally came at the behest of Chairman Mao Zedong, Defense Minister Lin Piao, and other Chinese political leaders, and did not stem from the PLA itself, at least initially. It was possible only because the CPC itself was in such disarray that "the army was the only nationwide organization that could claim to be disciplined and reliable."[6] Following the death of Lin Piao in 1971 (after plans for a coup attempt were exposed), the PLA's involvement in high politics gradually waned and it reverted to its more traditional military role. There are other examples of the PLA's involvement in Chinese politics, such as in the succession struggle connected with Mao's death, but none are as dramatic as the Great Cultural Revolution, and all ended in the same way, with the military retreating from politics. One manifestation of the PLA's partiality for professionalism and political neutrality is the fact that top military officials have at least twice opposed moves by the Party to politicize the army. During the Great Leap Forward, Defense Minister P'eng Te'huai was dismissed (1959) for opposing Party efforts to politicize the military. Mao's attempt to pull the army into politics on the eve of the Cultural Revolution was likewise opposed by Lo Jui-ch'ing, chief of staff of the army in 1963. He, too, was dismissed.

Ellis Joffe has attributed the PLA's traditional quiescence in politics to the "integrative power of modern Chinese nationalism," which causes the army and many other elements of Chinese society to place a high value on national unity. This in turn stems both from an aversion to warlordism, China's bane at earlier periods of its history, and from concern that China will once again become dependent on foreign powers and lose the capacity to act independently.[7] Another persistent tendency of the PLA has been regionalism, a problem that can be traced back for centuries in the military history of China.[8] China's individual field armies are geographically based and have tended to act somewhat independently of one another; tension erupts periodically between the field armies and the central command structure in Beijing. Partly to combat this tendency, the Party after 1967 appears to have deliberately rotated some military units and military officers from one province to another.

The PLA and the Events of Tiananmen Square
The PLA's historic role was replicated with surprising consistency during the internal crisis that led to the declaration of martial law and the military crackdown at Tiananmen Square in May and June 1989. The crisis saw military leaders pulled into politics, regional tensions surface within the military, and factional divisions within the political leadership played out in the military. Yet a military takeover was never a serious pros-

pect, and in the end, the military assumed its usual professional role, clearly subordinate to Party command.

The Tiananmen crisis began with the death of Hu Yaobang
on April 15, 1989. Hu had been a popular leader among
China's students, and his death elicited student demonstrations in Beijing that quickly grew in size and spread to other
parts of the country. By May 4, more than 100,000 workers
and students were marching in the streets of Beijing, and by
mid-May, at the time of the Gorbachev summit meeting, one
million demonstrators were in the streets, posing an unprecedented challenge to China's Communist leadership. Some
clashes had occurred between police and students in April, but
the first serious attempt to use the military to contain the
growing crisis came on May 19, when Premier Li Peng and
President Yang Shangkun announced after a meeting of top
officials that martial law would be imposed in many parts of
Beijing. By this date, some troops from the 27th Army in
Shanxi were already being moved to Beijing; this army was
regarded as a reliable ally of President Yang.[9]

The imposition of martial law in Beijing was accompanied
by a serious factional struggle within the Communist Party
leadership about how to deal with the crisis and whether to
bring in the PLA. A main opponent of using the military was
Zhao Ziyang, general secretary of the CPC and first vice chairman of the Central Military Commission (CMC); he reportedly
was supported by another Politburo member, Hu Qili. Zhao
had advocated a conciliatory approach, both in public and in a
meeting of the Politburo Standing Committee on May 16, at
the height of the student demonstrations. Zhao's position was
opposed by a coalition of Party elders and conservatives. Only
one day after presenting his position, Zhao was relieved of his
responsibilities as Party secretary by the full Politburo. (Zhao's
formal removal did not occur until late June; Hu Qili also lost
his place on the Standing Committee of the Politburo.)

The exact position taken in this struggle by China's top
military leaders is unknown. Unconfirmed reports suggest that
some regional military commanders voiced opposition to the
declaration of martial law. Deng is said to have held a stormy
meeting with commanders from the Beijing, Lanzhou, and

Guangzhou military regions, and many military officers signed a petition opposing the use of force against the people.[10] There is reason to believe, however, that most of the top military leadership at the political center supported Deng's hard-line position. Zhao had never won the trust or favor of the military, and he had been made a scapegoat for numerous problems in the armed forces, including low morale, poor living conditions, and the slow pace of modernization. Zhao was also blamed by the military for reductions in the ratio of China's defense expenditures to other spending.

As for Deng, he had ensured the personal loyalty of the PLA by having handpicked most of China's top generals, the majority of whom (9 of 17) came either from his power base in the Second Field Army or from his own unit, the 129th Division. Among them was the defense minister, Qin Jiwei, who remained loyal to Deng although he was known to favor reform. Within China's top military leadership there was a smaller faction that was not closely associated with Deng and that apparently resented his favoritism toward the Second Field Army. What position they took in the decision of mid-May is less certain, but they are likely to have been among those who opposed martial law. Both the dismissal of Zhao and the subsequent declaration of martial law were thus the result of an internal power struggle in which the conservative leadership, both political and military, won out. By May 25, the struggle within the Politburo was resolved, and six out of seven of the PRC's regional commands had declared their allegiance to the martial law decree. Significantly, the Beijing Military District did not publicly support the decree, which may in part explain why the leadership summoned troops from outlying provinces.[11]

From this time until June 4, a tense standoff occurred between PLA troops that had been summoned to Beijing and the thousands of students and workers then controlling the streets. Students and Beijing citizens built barricades, harassed troops, and prevented their movement into the center of the city by massing in the streets. They also confronted military soldiers and officers with questions about why they wanted to repress a democratic movement, leading many soldiers to pledge that they would never fire on the people. These two weeks were undoubtedly an extremely difficult period for the PLA, which faced growing unrest in its own ranks over the prospects of a possible military crackdown. The revered status of intellectuals in Chinese society made the dilemma particularly acute. During this period, several regional military commanders reportedly warned against the use of force and refused to attend a meeting with President Yang Shangkun.[12] Meanwhile, Western observers speculated about whether the PLA would obey orders to use force against the demonstrators.

All doubt was erased in the early morning hours of June 4, when tens of thousands of PLA troops captured the center of Beijing, expelling protestors from Tiananmen Square by force. The action in Beijing was accompanied by a military crackdown throughout the country. Before peace was restored, hundreds of Chinese citizens, including many students, had been killed and many hundreds more injured or arrested. A number of soldiers also perished in the ensuing street battles.[13] The willingness of Chinese troops to fire on students and workers outraged public opinion in China and badly damaged the prestige of the PLA. One Chinese journalist told the *New York Times* that "we thought this kind of thing only happened during the reign of the corrupt government of the Kuomintang. Yet this happened in our People's Republic. The troops and the police, they are supposed to be our brothers."[14]

On June 5, one day after the crackdown began, the Headquarters of the General Staff and the General Political Department of the Armed Forces issued a letter to the troops who were enforcing martial law congratulating them on a great victory over counterrevolutionary forces. This was clearly intended as a signal that the top military leadership fully supported the repressive action. Further evidence of civilian-military solidarity on the need for a violent crackdown came when Deng delivered his famous speech of June 9 to the military commanders who had conducted the operation. Present at the speech were prominent uniformed members of the CMC, including the minister of defense, General Qin Jiwei; Generals Hong Xuezhi and Liu Huaqing, CMC deputy secretary generals; the director of the General Logistics Department, General Zhao Nanqi; and the chief of the General Staff, General Chi Haotian.

The military operation at Tiananmen Square represented the first time since 1949 that army units from outside Beijing's own military garrison had been sent to the capital city. The 27th Army apparently bore the brunt of the fighting in the central city itself, but the more than 150,000 troops that were mobilized came from all seven military regions of the country and included forces from 13 out of 24 group armies, the regionally based corps that are the largest subdivisions of Chinese ground forces. By mobilizing forces from all regions of the country in Beijing, China's political and military leadership may have intended not only to demonstrate its unity, but to ensure that the regionalist tendencies of specific armies would be submerged in a common effort. No regional commander would be able to claim that his forces did not participate in or support the operation. Despite this precaution, however, there were numerous reports that the 38th Army refused to participate in the crackdown and even exchanged gunfire with the 27th Army.[15] These reports have never been confirmed, but developments in the PLA during the months after June 4 suggest very strongly that the leadership of the 38th Army was indeed disloyal to the central government and that problems of military obedience abounded throughout the armed forces during and in the aftermath of the crackdown.

Within days of the crackdown, the commander of the 38th Army, Major General Xu Qinxian, was arrested for refusing to order his troops into Beijing. Another commander, Major General Lu Xiangsheng of the 28th Army, may also have been removed for displaying a reluctance to deploy his forces in the operation.[16] There were signs of concern over the loyalty of the Guangdong Military Region, which was the last region to send a message of support to the Central Committee in Beijing after the crackdown. There were also reports that operational restrictions were placed on air force units in that region and that a former commander of the region, You Taizhong, was dispatched to Canton shortly after June 4 to seek assurances about the loyalty of the regional commanders to the central government.[17]

Problems of discipline and loyalty were probably not confined only to specific army units or military regions. Evidence suggests that a more pervasive problem affected the armed forces as a whole. At the rank and file level, hundreds or even thousands of soldiers are believed to have resisted or disobeyed orders to engage in battle with civilians, and many were reportedly under investigation even months after the crackdown had occurred.[18] In November, an enlarged plenary session of the CMC's Discipline Inspection Commission took place in Beijing. By this time, the political situation had settled down, and regular police had replaced the PLA troops occupying parts of Beijing. The chairman of the commission, Guo Linxiang, had this to say about the unrest of the previous June:

> During the struggle to stop upheavals and suppress the counterrevolutionary rebellion, Armed Forces discipline inspection commissions acted firmly and unequivocally in upholding Party principles and *they withstood a formidable challenge.*[19]

Guo also stressed that the Discipline Inspection Commission faced higher demands than ever before, that "the task before us is rather arduous, and the responsibility on our shoulders is heavy." He emphasized the importance of opposing "decentralism and the practice of each going his own way," and stressed that the army must be strictly loyal and show "iron discipline" in enforcing the decisions of the Central Committee.[20]

During the months following the crackdown, ideological education in the army received renewed prominence, with constant emphasis on the subordination of the military to Party authority. There was a crackdown on corrupt practices in the army, and a number of middle-level commanders were dismissed for violations of discipline or other "mistakes." An expanded program of military and political education for university students was also introduced.[21] In December, an All-Army Political Work Conference was held in Beijing devoted to the theme of strengthening the army's political work "under the new situation" and ensuring "that the army is forever qualified politically." The conference produced a 10-point document, the thrust of which was aptly summarized in Point Six: "Guarantee that the barrel of the gun is held in the hands of politically reliable people."[22]

Further evidence that the problems of discipline in the army were more serious than initially realized came early in 1990, after martial law had been formally lifted. Six of China's seven regional military commanders were shuffled, and a number of officers who played a prominent role in the June crackdown were promoted. Lieutenant General Zhu Dunfa, deputy commander of the Shenyang Military Region, which had responded quickly to the summons for help from Beijing, was promoted and made head of the less reliable Canton region. Significantly, both the commander and the political commissar of the Beijing Military Region, Lieutenant Generals Zhou Yibing and Liu Zhenhua, were replaced, probably because of their reluctance to support martial law as well as the disloyalty of some troops under their command (including the 38th Army). Their replacements were considered to be closely allied with hard-line political leaders. The new political commissar, Major General Zhang Gong, had been the military spokesman who defended the crackdown in June and denied that any civilians had been killed at Tiananmen Square.[23]

These developments should not be interpreted as representing a crisis in Chinese civil-military relations. To the contrary, the highest military leadership of the country appears to have fully supported (and perhaps even encouraged) the military crackdown undertaken in June, and senior military officers headed up the effort to impose greater discipline and ideological education on the army in the aftermath of the crisis. In short, the army's inherent professionalism triumphed over its tendency toward regional factionalism. The military intervention in Chinese domestic politics took place at the behest of the Party, and the leading role of the Party was never seriously challenged at the top, despite widespread problems with discipline in specific army units.

In a crisis brought about by the rapid pace of China's economic and political development, the PLA manifested the characteristic qualities for which it had been known since 1949—albeit not without signs of serious internal crisis. It is yet too early to speak of a post-Communist China, but the professionalism of the PLA suggests that it will remain aloof from politics until it is again called on for support by the Party leadership or until a profound political crisis divides the Party into competing factions. In the latter instance, the regionalism of the military may surface, and factions in the political leadership could again play themselves out in the armed forces.[24] The crackdown of 1989 did not in any way resolve the internal social tensions building in China as a result of its rapid development. Nor is the post-Deng succession picture any less uncertain. It may be only a few years, then, before the political loyalty of the military is again put to a test.

Vietnam and North Korea

Both Vietnam and North Korea have strenuously resisted the tide of change affecting Communist regimes around the world. Neither has experienced serious internal crisis or serious problems of any kind in civil-military relations. Yet social and economic pressures are building in each country, and these could yet lead to major changes.

Vietnam

In Vietnam, the demobilization of thousands of troops following the September 1989 withdrawal from Cambodia contributed to rising unemployment in the country. After serving many years in the military, soldiers find it difficult to adjust to civilian life. The army newspaper *Quan Doi Nhan Dan* even estimated that as of 1990 only 7 percent of all troops demobilized since 1976 had found permanent full-time employment; of the remaining, 25 percent had found only part-time work and 68 percent were jobless.[25] The tens of thousands of troops who served for years in the southern part of the country also pose a special problem: having seen the relative prosperity of the South, they are sometimes disillusioned with the austere life of the North. Signs of this discontent appeared in 1983, when a group of military officers serving in the South, all Party members, formed a private interest organization, the Club of Foreign Resistance Fighters. The organization was headed by General Tran Van Tra, the former military governor of Saigon. For years this organization attempted to win official recognition from the authorities in Hanoi, meanwhile lobbying for greater democratization of Party procedures. In March 1990, the organization finally received official recognition as the

"Vietnam Veterans Association," perhaps because the regime realized that its growing body of military veterans posed a potentially serious social problem if not handled carefully.[26]

The magnitude of its veteran problem reflects the fact that for more than 40 years Vietnam has been one of the most militarized countries in the world. Following the war with the United States, the anticipated demobilization of the People's Army of Vietnam (PAVN) never occurred: the army was called on first to occupy, "reeducate," and rehabilitate the South, then to invade and occupy Cambodia, then to deal with an incessant threat from China. As a result, the PAVN (including militia) has nearly 2.9 million soldiers, a remarkable 4 percent of the country's total population. This gives Vietnam nearly as many soldiers as China (where only 0.3 percent of the population is in arms). The high degree of mobilization, coupled with what Douglas Pike has called "the integrated, symbiotic relationship of military to Party," accounts for the absence "over the years [of] few truly serious tensions . . . between Party and military." Perhaps more than any other Communist (or non-Communist) government in the world, the Party and the army in Vietnam are linked inextricably. Yet this has not prevented the Party from constantly emphasizing its "absolute," "direct," and "complete" control over the army.[27]

The burden of sustaining such a large standing army has contributed to Vietnam's severe economic problems. In 1988, inflation reached nearly 700 percent and unemployment topped 20 percent. Severe austerity measures introduced by the government in March 1989 helped to bring inflation down but caused a cash shortage throughout the Vietnamese economy, making it impossible sometimes for even large state-owned factories to pay their workers or taxes. In 1989 Vietnam also began exporting sizable quantities of rice for the first time in 30 years; this led, however, to shortages at home that bordered on famine in some provinces.[28]

In the face of such challenges, Vietnam's Communist leaders displayed understandable defensiveness toward the political developments of 1989 in Eastern Europe. At the Seventh Plenum of the Central Committee in August 1989, Party chief Nguyen Van Linh spoke of the "very high level of unanimity" of the Party in rejecting "bourgeois liberalization, pluralism, political plurality and multi-opposition parties aimed at denying Marxism-Leninism."[29] While acknowledging the need for some reforms at home, he also accused Western governments of trying to undermine socialism worldwide. Hanoi's defensiveness may be compounded by the fact that it is in the middle of a prolonged succession struggle, the beginning of a crucial generational transition.

The combination of forces at work in Vietnam suggests that the country will not long be able to continue its high level of militarization and political uniformity. At some point, reforms will become inevitable. Introducing them may spawn internal crisis. The military is certain to be reduced in size, and its relationship with a new generation of civilian leaders may also change. It is known that top generals were unhappy with the regime's "no win" policy in Cambodia and were concerned that Vietnam's economic problems and dependence on the USSR for high-technology weaponry would hinder its ability to defend itself over the long run.[30] Such concerns may well be magnified manyfold as Vietnam's glacial political system gives way to change. That will be the time to watch for a crisis in civil-military relations in Vietnam.

North Korea

North Korea as of the end of 1990 remained, if anything, even more frozen in time than Vietnam. "Although the 1980s have seen convulsive changes elsewhere in the Communist bloc, North Korea closed the decade showing no indication that any change to basic state politics was being contemplated."[31] Kim Il-sung was reelected as president for a four-year term in May 1990 with the usual 100 percent margin of victory, and the official rhetoric of the regime shows little sign of adapting to the age of *glasnost.* Economically, North Korea's growth rate has stagnated but remains slightly positive (perhaps 2 percent in 1989, down from 9.7 percent at the beginning of the decade).

The one development that may portend future change is the opening of official talks between North and South Korea. In 1989 the countries initiated a thaw in their commercial relations and also began negotiations on opening high-level talks. These led in September 1990 to a visit to Seoul by North Korean Premier Yon Hyong Muk and seven senior officials for

the first of a series of "premier talks." South Korea recipro-
cated with a visit by Prime Minister Kang Young Hoon in
October 1990. Little progress was made in these talks, but
they pointed toward a possible détente between the two countries that might open North Korea to potential liberalizing
influences from the South. The subsequent decision by North
Korea to relinquish its opposition to each country seeking
separate membership in the United Nations further confirmed
a modest political thaw in the North.

Like Vietnam, North Korea is highly militarized, with
roughly 5 percent of its population under arms. It is also
reported to have under way an intensive and well-funded
program to develop nuclear weapons, a prospect that gives
nightmares to U.S. and South Korean military planners. In
1989, North Korea claimed to have reduced its military forces
by 150,000 troops in the course of recent years, but according
to Western estimates, the size of its army actually increased to
over one million, including 930,000 ground troops.[32] If a
genuine rapprochement develops between the two Koreas, it
will become difficult to justify maintaining so large an army.
Reduction in force may then become an issue between civilian
and military leaders.

In October 1983, the North Korean military was involved
in a terrorist bombing that killed four South Korean ministers
in Rangoon. After two North Korean army officers confessed
the crime to Burmese authorities, the official under whose
authority the operation had nominally fallen, Kim Jung Rin,
was quietly demoted (he returned to the inner leadership
circle as a member of the Party Secretariat in 1990). Whether
senior military leaders also suffered as a result of the fiasco is
not known but is likely. Since that time, the only evidence
hinting of possible disagreement between civilian and military
leaders occurred following the February 1988 dismissal of Oh
Guk Ryol, chief of the General Staff, when his seat on the
Politburo was left vacant, thus reducing overall military repre-
sentation at the top of the North Korean hierarchy.[33] (Some
observers speculated that the omission of Oh Jim Wu, minister
of the armed forces, from a cabinet list issued in May 1990 was
a sign that he, too, had fallen from favor, but his inclusion on a

separate list as vice chairman of the National Defense Commission suggested this may have been an unintentional oversight.)[34]

North Korea at present seems as far from abandoning or even reforming communism as perhaps any regime in the world. But with Kim Il-sung approaching 80, it faces a major generational transition in the near future that, coupled with its economic problems, could lead to pressures for political change. These in turn may affect the military. Should a post-Communist order eventually emerge in North Korea, it may of course lead in short order to reunification with the South, along the German pattern. But if North Korea retains its separate identity while abandoning Marxist-Leninist ideology, it will likely field armed forces much smaller than at present. Such a force would probably revert to the traditional nationalistic role of most Asian armies in the post-colonial era: it would see its primary mission as preserving the independence of the country from foreign, particularly Japanese and U.S., influences.

The Revolutionary Armed Forces of Cuba

As in China, Vietnam, and North Korea, there is in Cuba a close historical link between the army and the Communist state. Both institutions originated from the small rebel army that landed on the coast of Cuba in December 1956 and overthrew the regime of Fulgencio Batista in 1959. "There was no real issue of civilian control over the armed forces in those early years of the revolution. Those who held administrative control *were* the armed forces."[35] The Matos affair (October 1959) and the rapid growth of the Revolutionary Armed Forces (Fuerzas Armadas Revolucionarias, or FAR) eventually led the new regime to introduce formal political training and controls into the Cuban military. These were resisted strongly by the officer corps of the FAR, who saw them as a threat to military discipline.[36] Beginning in 1970, however, as a result of the reorganization of the Cuban political system, the close link between the officer corps and the top political leadership became weaker. This led after 1974 to the political education program of the armed forces being significantly expanded.

The reputation of Cuba's armed forces soared in the 1970s when thousands of troops were sent abroad to perform their "internationalist duty" in Angola, Ethiopia, and elsewhere. At the peak of this deployment, which lasted throughout the 1980s, more than 50,000 Cuban troops were serving overseas, a remarkable feat for a country of only 10 million. By 1990, a total of 2,289 of these troops had perished in combat or by illness and accidents.[37] The hero of the Angolan and Ethiopian operations was General Arnaldo Ochoa Sánchez, who became perhaps the most decorated and heralded military hero in the history of Communist Cuba and who was said to be second in popularity only to Fidel Castro himself. His stature also explains why Cuban society was so shocked by the revelation in June 1989 that he had been arrested for "serious acts of corruption and mismanagement of economic funds."

Ochoa was arrested on June 12, 1989, along with 3 other officers of the Revolutionary Armed Forces and 11 officers from the Ministry of the Interior (which controls Cuba's police forces). After being stripped of his Party positions, Ochoa was turned over to a military tribunal consisting of 47 generals and was put on trial in a televised proceeding with all the trappings of a Stalinist show trial. The trial was the most closely watched political event in Cuba since 1959. The principal charge was international drug-trafficking, but the defendants were also accused of numerous acts of corruption, theft of state property, "immorality," and "high treason." In a rambling speech to the court, Cuban Defense Minister Raúl Castro claimed that there had been suspicions about Ochoa's conduct as early as 1970 and that he had been reprimanded or corrected more often than any other senior military officer.[38] Ochoa confessed to all charges, and he and three other officers were executed by firing squad on July 13, barely a month after their arrest.

Ochoa's execution was followed by a thorough shake-up in the Ministry of the Interior, including the arrest of an additional three generals at the ministry. Among them was Division General José Abrantes Fernández, the former minister of the interior who had been dismissed from his post shortly following Ochoa's arrest. Although there were no further executions, all of the defendants were tried in military courts and given lengthy prison sentences. Numerous lesser officials were also put on trial, so that eventually 23 persons at the Ministry of the Interior were accused of crimes.

The Ochoa affair provoked widespread speculation that more than drug-trafficking was involved. The *Wall Street Journal* saw it as a cover-up for Castro, who himself was thought to have been involved in drug-trafficking; the *Christian Science Monitor* and *Newsweek* both interpreted it as a political trial, with policy differences and political rivalries hidden behind the facade of a criminal trial; one U.S. academic speculated in the *Wall Street Journal* that Ochoa had become too popular, thus arousing Castro's envy.[39] Plausible though such speculations may seem, there is not enough hard evidence to confirm any of them with certainty. Most observers agreed that the charges against Ochoa and his accomplices were basically accurate, but there was great skepticism that their activities could have continued so long without coming to Castro's attention. It was widely believed (and testified to at the trial by one of the defendants) that the "highest levels" of the Cuban government knew of the drug-trafficking. The United States for years had claimed that high Cuban officials were involved in smuggling drugs, and one of the officers (Admiral Aldo Santamaria) who served on the tribunal that condemned Ochoa had even been indicted for drug-smuggling in a U.S. court in 1982.

It is known that General Ochoa's home in Havana had become a gathering point for veterans of the African wars who were unhappy with the conditions they found in Cuba after years abroad. These veterans had numerous grievances about the military bureaucracy headed by Raúl Castro, and Ochoa is believed to have encouraged talk about major reforms of the Communist system. One theory, therefore, is that Castro knew and even approved of the drug-smuggling and only used it against the generals when their political loyalty came into question. "By executing Ochoa and Antonio de la Guardia, Castro warned his subordinates that mere talk about reforms would be regarded as treason, no matter what position advocates of changes would occupy in the armed forces, the government, or the Party."[40]

This theory must be balanced against indications that the Ochoa affair did concern individual crimes or acts of political disloyalty rather than a larger political struggle between civilian and military leaders. There were few signs, for example, of any crisis in Cuban civil-military relations following the incident. To the contrary, when the Ministry of the Interior was reorganized, the guidelines for doing so were drafted by military officers at the Ministry of Revolutionary Armed Forces, and the Central Committee meeting that endorsed the changes was attended by a full panoply of Cuba's top officers. Likewise, at an Extraordinary Plenum of the Central Committee in February 1990, Brigadier General Sergio Pérez Lezcano was elected a full member of the committee and appointed to the Party Secretariat. More personnel changes occurred in the Party establishment (Politburo and Secretariat) at this plenum than in the Committee for Defense of the Revolution. The plenum did mention the Ochoa affair as one reason for a continuing "rectification" campaign to "revitalize" and "perfect" the Party, but this campaign was aimed primarily at mass organizations and Party work, not at the FAR.[41]

Tempting though it is to see the Ochoa affair as part of the larger pattern of crisis in Communist militaries around the world, there is insufficient evidence to support this hypothesis. All the same, Cuba will face serious strains in the future that could affect the tenor of civil-military relations. The country is in appalling economic shape, compounded recently by a two-million-ton shortfall in deliveries of Soviet oil. External debt has reached nearly $7 billion, with only $87.9 million in hard-currency reserves on hand by mid-1989. Housing, public works, communications, and other infrastructure are falling apart, and widespread rationing of basic commodities has been introduced. The collapse of communism in Eastern Europe, the electoral defeat of the Sandinista government in Nicaragua in February 1990, and the opening of a U.S. government broadcasting effort aimed at Cuba have all placed the Caribbean country on the ideological defensive. The return since 1989 of more than 31,000 troops from Africa will also pose unprecedented problems for the FAR and the Cuban government. These soldiers will need housing and employment if they are not to become a politically restless interest group whose existence could stimulate tensions between the military and the civil authorities. Although it is true, as one Western scholar has written, that "a traditional military coup in Cuba today is unlikely," civil-military tensions will probably increase in the future.[42]

A Third World Triad: Nicaragua, Angola, and Ethiopia

The cases of Nicaragua, Angola, and Ethiopia deserve brief mention as examples of how the larger crisis of communism has spread even to the radical allies of the USSR in the Third World. All three countries during the 1980s were styled "Communist" by the Western press, although in fact they did not establish the full panoply of Communist institutions characteristic of the political systems discussed above. More accurately, they should be described as Marxist-Leninist regimes allied with the Soviet Union. Their political evolution since 1989 nevertheless mirrors the larger crisis of the Communist world.[43]

In Nicaragua, the Sandinista government of Daniel Ortega Saavedra yielded power in April 1990 following an unexpected electoral defeat the preceding February. Upon entering office, the new president, Violeta Chamorro, ended conscription and announced drastic reductions in the size of the Nicaraguan army. In a move that generated much controversy, she also retained Humberto Ortega (brother of the former president) as chief of the armed forces. The Sandinistas also retained control of the security police and the labor unions. All this made it possible for Ortega to carry out his threat of governing the country "from below." In the first 18 months after Chamorro's government took over, the Sandinistas have caused periodic disruptions through strikes, police raids, and the threat of military force. Most recently, Ortega has threatened to resume civil war if the government goes forward with plans to repeal the so-called La Piñata, the massive transfer of public property (including 10,000 homes and one million acres of land) to Sandinista hands, that occurred at the transition of regimes.

Thus, since April 1990, Nicaragua has been in the unusual situation of being a non-Communist country with an armed forces controlled by a Marxist-Leninist party. In July 1991, Chamorro confirmed that she would continue to retain

Humberto Ortega as commander of the armed forces, a move her advisers described as a "balancing game" but one resented by many of her supporters. Chamorro's election helped tame the ideological and political strife that rent Nicaragua during its years of civil war, but the result has been a government that embodies those tensions in its very structure. Until and unless the armed forces of Nicaragua are brought under the control of its elected authorities, the situation in the country will remain unstable at best and the military a constant factor in politics.

Angola since 1975 has been ruled by the Popular Movement for the Liberation of Angola (MPLA), the Marxist party that came to power on the strength of Soviet arms and Cuban troops following the withdrawal of Portugal from its African colony. Its command of Angola has been tenuous, however. For 16 years it engaged in a continual civil war with the National Union for Total Independence of Angola (UNITA). With the aid of Cuban troops, the MPLA maintained control of the capital city of Luanda and of the major urban centers and highways, while UNITA, aided first by South Africa and later by the United States, held sway throughout much of the countryside, particularly in the South. The war came to an end in May 1991, following the signing of a cease-fire and peace agreement between the MPLA and UNITA that was brokered by both the United States and the Soviet Union. As part of this agreement, Angolan President José Eduardo Dos Santos agreed to the establishment of a multiparty system, a single armed forces, and free elections in the fall of 1992.

Angola thus faces the problem of integrating two armies that have been at war with one another for 16 years. This dilemma may prove even more vexing than the situation in Nicaragua, where the Sandinista armed forces at least remain intact within a non-Sandinista government, or in Ethiopia, where a rebel army has won complete victory and assumed direct control of the country. The price of military stalemate in Angola is likely to be a military divided within itself. The potential for future coups or a breakdown of the peace agreement in such a situation must be rated very high.

In Ethiopia, Tigrean and Eritrean rebels overthrew the government of Mengistu Haile-Mariam in May 1991, following years of civil war. Mengistu was a lieutenant colonel in the

Ethiopian military when he came to power in 1977 after an interfactional struggle within the Dergue, the military council that ruled Ethiopia after the fall of Haile Selassie. Mengistu's government during most of his 14 years in power was dominated by the military rather than by a political party, as would be the usual rule in Communist countries. Not until September 1987 did a civilian government (still headed by Mengistu) replace the military administration that had ruled Ethiopia since 1975. Even after this government was in place, the Ethiopian military continued to hold great sway in political affairs, acting as the arbiter of internal disputes over policy.

In May 1989, officers of the Second Army based in Asmara mutinied against the government, demanding political reforms and an end to the wars in Eritrea and Tigre. At the same time and for essentially the same reasons, the armed forces chief of staff, Major General Merid Negusie, and the air force commander, Major General Amha Desta, attempted to stage a coup in Addis Ababa. Security forces loyal to Mengistu managed to prevent the coup after much bloodshed in the city. Heavy fighting was also required to put down the mutiny of the Second Army. At least 27 senior army officers died in the fighting in Addis Ababa, 400 officers were arrested, and a dozen generals were later executed. The resultant demoralization of the armed forces, already weary after years of civil war, probably contributed to the collapse of Mengistu's regime the next year. One piece of evidence that Mengistu realized his weakness after the coup attempt was his dramatic reversal of policy just one month later in agreeing to open peace talks with the Eritrean People's Liberation Front. Mengistu also announced plans for major political and economic reforms the following March in a desperate attempt to bolster the legitimacy of his collapsing regime.

The defeat of Mengistu was possible only because the Ethiopian military had lost the will to fight and had little commitment to a regime that had ruined the country economically. Even after Mengistu left Ethiopia, with rebel forces just miles outside the capital, the new leader, Tesfaye Gebre-Kidan (a general and former defense minister) admitted that he had no control of the army and would let the rebels enter Addis Ababa without a fight. His announcement sparked another brief, irrelevant coup attempt by angry soldiers just before the rebel forces took the capital, making both the Ethiopian government and army irrelevant. The resultant victory of the Eritrean and Tigrean rebels over the Ethiopian army is a very rare historical case of secessionist forces capturing a political center in order to realize their objectives. As such, it differs diametrically from the cases of Yugoslavia and the USSR, where secessionist forces have no hope of or interest in taking the political center.

The common threads in the experience of Nicaragua, Angola, and Ethiopia were, first, the fact that all three regimes were at war virtually throughout their existence, and second, the failure of all three regimes to create professional military forces clearly subordinate to civilian authority. Constant warfare brought military leadership to the fore, which contributed to the weakening of civilian (and where applicable, Party) control. It also strained the resources, angered the citizenry, and threatened the political legitimacy of all three governments. When Soviet support was withdrawn or reduced following the accession of Gorbachev, these governments proved incapable of surviving as Marxist-Leninist states. In Cuba, Vietnam, China, and North Korea, by contrast, revolutionary armies were made subordinate to Party control early in their political development (and only Vietnam of these countries endured years of ceaseless warfare). Mao was wrong. There are times when power does not flow out of the barrel of a gun. Sometimes, relying too much on the gun barrel only hastens the loss of power.

5
Conclusions: Toward a Post-Communist Military Order

Three main factors appear to shape the evolution of military organizations in Communist countries undergoing systemic crisis: military professionalism, internal social trends, and nationalism. *Military professionalism* strongly mitigates any tendency of senior officers to intervene directly in politics, while *internal social trends* cause officers and soldiers to adapt gradually to the changes occurring in society as a whole. The role of *nationalism* is more complex. Most commonly it serves as a substitute for ideology, causing armies to respond to systemic crisis by reverting to traditional patterns and values; in multinational states, such as the USSR and Yugoslavia, it can also be a politically divisive force straining at the fabric of the state. The professional officer corps will resist nationalism's centrifugal force in such instances.

Military professionalism has meant that where Communist governments have been replaced by non-Communist governments, the armed forces have rapidly shed their ideological veneer and switched their allegiance to the new regime. Communist military officers are military first and Communist only second. Decades of ideological indoctrination have proved of little effect against the larger forces of professionalism and social change. These rapid switches of allegiance also manifest the force of nationalism. The loyalty of Communist armies is less to the Communist state than to the nation-state; therefore, when new governments represent genuinely nationalist forces, the military will usually support them.

This line of analysis would suggest that military coups in Communist countries are extremely unlikely to succeed, even in periods of crisis and transition. In the USSR, military professionalism led many senior officers to resist the anti-Gorbachev coup of August 1991. The small number of officers directly implicated in that plot (which included government and police officials as well) suggests that decades of indoctrination against military intervention in politics has paid off. The one exception to this rule would be countries (largely in the Third World) that do not establish fully professional armies or implement effective political controls. To date, at least, the only true military coup that has occurred anywhere in the Communist world was in Ethiopia in May 1989, and it failed. Nicaragua and Angola remain likely prospects for a military coup. Elsewhere, the prospects are much smaller. In Romania the armed forces did act directly against the state, yet this was not a coup but rather a case of the military joining a popular uprising. The same social forces that caused the popular uprising in the first place also swung the loyalty of the military in support of a revolt that almost the entire country welcomed. The declaration of martial law in Poland also was not a coup per se, but a military operation conducted with the support of the Party and in its behalf.

This conclusion requires two caveats, however. First, it is clear that the more protracted an internal crisis is, the more likely the military is to be pulled into political involvement. That happened in Poland from 1980 to 1989, where the military gradually assumed more and more of the functions of state. And it clearly has been the trend in the USSR and Yugoslavia since 1989. The sheer rapidity with which communism collapsed in the rest of Eastern Europe (coupled with popular aversion to the regimes in power) may be one reason why military organizations there adapted so easily to the changed situation. A reactionary backlash had no time to gain force.

The second caveat is that there are limits to the restraining force of military professionalism. Military professionalism does not prevent civil-military tensions and disputes from arising— it only keeps them within certain bounds. Tensions are to be expected in a time of profound change and crisis; the question is under what circumstances these will escalate into violence. The major instances of civil-military strife examined in this study did not derive from ideological differences but from the military's attempts to defend its professional prerogatives, public prestige, and priority in the national budget against the inevitable encroachments that occur in times of economic and social crisis. Military officers can tolerate ideological change.

Sharp cuts in the defense budget, however, or challenges to deeply held military values are another matter entirely. Thus, if a military coup does occur in a Communist country, it will probably be aimed less at saving communism than at saving the military. This may have been the motivation of Dmitrii Yazov and the handful of military officers involved in the August 1991 Soviet coup.

The force of nationalism has been particularly crucial in cases where Communist regimes have disintegrated or undergone prolonged crisis. In such instances, military organizations have fallen back on their historical traditions, values, and patterns of behavior; nationalism proves stronger and more enduring than ideology. In countries such as Yugoslavia, Czechoslovakia, and the USSR, where ethnic divisions threaten political unity, the state-oriented nationalism of the armed forces has been a stabilizing and unifying force. In general, armies are loyal to the nation-state rather than to the parochial nationalism of its constituent parts. Both loyalties can coexist, however, within a single army. The senior officer corps of the Soviet Union, for example, manifests a strong determination to preserve the Soviet federation. This is much less true, however, of the Soviet rank and file, who are strongly influenced by the social trends and nationalisms of their home republics.

These general conclusions highlight overall trends and tendencies. They do not apply uniformly to every country or region. In fact, the case studies suggest that there are at least three categories of Communist countries to consider in examining civil-military relations. These categories derive from the historical origins and background of the armed forces in given countries. The first category would encompass what might be called the co-opted traditional armies of Eastern Europe. These are armies on whom communist ideology was imposed in the aftermath of World War II. Here the commitment to ideology is very weak, traditional values are strong, and the military is strongly affected by public opinion and trends. As we have seen, the transition from Communist rule to non-Communist governments in these countries took place with almost no resistance from the military. Subsequent reforms and budget cuts have elicited some grumbling among military officers but have not led to any serious civil-military strife.

The second category would include those countries where the rise of a revolutionary army was inextricably linked with the historical origins of the Communist state. China, Vietnam, North Korea, and Cuba all fall into this category. These countries remain firmly Communist, so it is premature to speak of a post-Communist order emerging in any of them. They possess genuinely revolutionary armies, armies that arose as the result of Communist revolution and whose officer corps did not inherit many of the traditions or values of the *anciens régimes* that they defeated. Where revolutionary armies exist, both the ideological bond between the army and the Party and the interpersonal connections at the top appear to be stronger and more enduring than in other Communist states. This may partly explain why civil-military strife is less prevalent in these countries, even when they are undergoing serious crises. The ideological commitment of officers in these armies may make them less subject to the pressures of public opinion and prevailing social trends. These external factors may still play a role in their behavior (as in the military factionalism in China in June 1989), but their sense of military professionalism is reinforced by an ideological affinity and commitment not found in the armies of the former Soviet bloc.

The third category occupies the middle ground between the first two and shares some elements of each. The USSR and Yugoslavia belong to this last category. Both countries have armies with deep historical roots and traditions that predate the Communist era, but both armies were also directly involved in the initial triumph of socialist rule. Both armies have prospered under communism, and some of their most important traditions stem from World War II, when they fought against fascism and for communism. It is also of great significance that both countries are multinational federations in which ethnic and national divisions strain the viability of centralized rule. In these countries, the military sees itself as crucial to the survival and cohesion of the state. Ideological commitment in these armies is less than in the revolutionary armies of Asia and Cuba but greater than in the co-opted armies of Eastern Europe.

The case of Yugoslavia suggests that the evolution of such regimes may be the most volatile of all. The violence associated with Yugoslavia's transition to non-Communist rule does not bode well for the multinational Soviet Union, which faces similar strains though on a vastly larger scale. Historically, military rivalry between states and the existence of external threats have acted as internal unifying forces. This unifying effect is particularly valuable for heterogeneous societies and governments that have no natural base of legitimacy. The tensions of the cold war in a perverse way helped to maintain the cohesion of both Yugoslavia and the USSR, despite the multinational cleavages afflicting them. With their sense of external threat reduced and legitimizing ideology in rapid decline, it appears doubtful that their armed forces alone will retain the popular support and internal unity necessary to counterbalance such centrifugal forces. This is all the more true given that conscript armies themselves are not immune from nationalist fragmentation.

The real military threat to Communist rule in multinational states may not be direct military intervention—which implies decisive planning and execution—but rather the inexorable fragmentation and demoralization of armed forces whose ranks reflect the crisis of their societies. Hundreds of mid-level Soviet officers and enlisted men rallied to support Boris Yeltsin during the August 1991 coup attempt precisely because the anti-Communist and reformist trends of Soviet society had affected them also. Military organizations, however professional they may be, can never be isolated from larger societal trends. More than once this study has observed that Communist military officers are military first and Communist second. Recent events suggest that they are human before all else.

Notes

Introduction

1. See Dale Herspring and Ivan Volgyes, "The Military as an Agent of Political Socialization in Eastern Europe," *Armed Forces and Society* 3, no. 2 (Winter 1977): 249–269, and a special issue devoted to a review of this model, *Studies in Comparative Communism* 11, no. 3 (Autumn 1978); Timothy J. Colton, *Commissars, Commanders, and Civilian Authority: The Structure of Soviet Military Politics* (Cambridge: Harvard University Press, 1979); Roman Kolkowicz, "The Military," in H. Gordon Skilling and Franklyn Griffiths, eds., *Interest Groups in Soviet Politics* (Princeton, N.J.: Princeton University Press, 1971).

The developmental model proposed by Dale Herspring and Ivan Volgyes in the late 1970s was useful but proved of limited applicability for many countries. Other approaches, such as the participatory model proposed by Timothy Colton or the group theory approach of Roman Kolkowicz, also are of little help now, given the unprecedented nature of the crisis faced by socialist armed forces in the late 1980s.

2. Samuel P. Huntington, *The Soldier and the State: The Theory and Politics of Civil-Military Relations* (Cambridge: Harvard University Press, 1957), 8–18, 55–58, 65, 83–85.

3. Zbigniew Brzezinski, "Post-Communist Nationalism," *Foreign Affairs* 68, no. 5 (Winter 1989/1990): 1–25.

Chapter 1 — The Crisis of Socialist Armed Forces: Underlying Causes

1. Both CIA and official Soviet figures are taken from William T. Lee, "Trends in Soviet Military Outlays and Economic Priorities 1970–1988" (Washington, D.C.: U.S. Senate Committee on Foreign Relations, July 30, 1990), Table B-11.

2. *PlanEcon Report* 6 (July 13, 1990).

3. Figures on Eastern Europe are from *PlanEcon Report* 6 (March 28, 1990), (June 22, 1990), and (September 14, 1990).

4. On the debt crisis of the 1980s, see Gerald Fink and Kurt Mauler, "Hard Currency Position of CMEA Countries and

Yugoslavia" (Die Osterreichische Spar-Casse-Bank, Vienna, Austria, November 1988.)

5. International Institute for Strategic Studies, *The Military Balance 1989–90* (London: Brassey's for IISS, 1989); Richard F. Staar, ed., *1990 Yearbook on International Communist Affairs* (Stanford, Calif.: Hoover Institution Press, 1990), 78–79, 454; Central Intelligence Agency, *The World Factbook 1989* (Washington, D.C., May 1989), 328.

6. CIA, *World Factbook 1989;* Far Eastern Economic Review, *The Asia Yearbook,* annual (Hong Kong, 1984 and 1990).

7. Far Eastern Economic Review, *Asia 1990 Yearbook,* 6, 113.

8. *Soviet Military Power* (Washington, D.C.: Department of Defense), 34.

9. Robin Remington, "Yugoslavia," in *1990 Yearbook on International Communist Affairs,* 462.

10. Ian Wilson and You Ji, "Leadership by 'Lines': China's Unresolved Succession," *Problems of Communism* 39 (January–February 1990): 42.

Chapter 2 — Crisis and Revolution: East European Armed Forces

1. Condoleezza Rice, "Warsaw Pact Reliability: The Czechoslovak People's Army (ČLA)," in Daniel N. Nelson, ed., *Soviet Allies: The Warsaw Pact and the Issue of Reliability* (Boulder, Colo.: Westview Press, 1984), 126.

2. Ibid., 131, 135–136.

3. Prague Television Service, October 4, 1989 (Foreign Broadcast Information Service [Eastern Europe], hereafter FBIS) and *Rude Pravo,* October 6, 1989 (FBIS).

4. *Rude Pravo,* October 18, 1989 (FBIS).

5. Moscow Domestic Service, November 24, 1989 (FBIS).

6. Radio Prague, December 6, 1989, and Četeka, December 6, 1989, provided courtesy of Radio Free Europe (RFE); Prague Domestic Service, December 6, 1989; Prague Domestic Service, December 19, 1989. In January, Vacek issued an order that the form of address in the military would be changed from "Comrade" to "Sir." Radio Prague, January 10, 1989 (RFE).

7. The first public denial came during a television interview with Defense Minister Vacek, December 6, 1989 (FBIS); the second was made by a military spokesman on December 19, 1989, who stated flatly that "all soldiers are firmly behind the present government of national accord." Prague Domestic Service, December 19, 1989 (FBIS).

8. Prague Domestic Service, December 19, 1989 (FBIS); Četeka, December 15, 1989 (RFE); *Reuter,* January 11 and 17, 1990 (RFE).

9. Jan Obrman, "Interview with First Deputy Chief of the General Staff," *Report on Eastern Europe,* July 20, 1990, pp. 14–17; Czechoslovak Domestic Service, September 6 and October 17–18, 1990 (RFE); other materials provided courtesy of RFE.

10. *Radio Free Europe/Radio Liberty (RFE/RL) Daily Report,* September 7, 1990; Tanjug, September 12, 1990 (RFE); Czechoslovak Domestic Service, October 18, 1990 (RFE); Civic Forum statement courtesy of RFE.

11. Czechoslovak Radio, January 13 and March 7, 1990 (RFE); Četeka, December 12, 1990 (RFE).

12. *New York Times,* February 20, 1991.

13. Ivan Volgyes, *The Political Reliability of the Warsaw Pact Armies: The Southern Tier* (Durham, N.C.: Duke University, 1982), 60.

14. *Magyar Hirlap,* August 8, 1988, cited in *Keesing's Record of World Events* (London: Longman, 1988), 36165.

15. Budapest MTI, September 17, 1989 (FBIS).

16. "Rumors of Military Intervention," Hungarian SR/13, September 1, 1989, *Radio Free Europe Research* (hereafter *RFER*).

17. Budapest MTI, September 20, 1989 (FBIS) and Budapest Television, September 28, 1990 (FBIS); Budapest MTI, October 2, 1989 (FBIS).

18. Hungarian SR/15, October 4, 1989, *RFER*.

19. Most of the changes were announced by Nemeth at a conference of army leaders; see Budapest Domestic Service, December 1, 1989 (FBIS). The Defense Ministry also held a news briefing that day to clarify the proposed reforms; see ibid. and Budapest MTI, December 1, 1989 (FBIS).

20. Zoltan D. Barany, "Major Reorganization of Hungary's Military Establishment," Research and Analysis Division (RAD) Background Report/230, December 28, 1989, *RFER.*

21. For the background to this issue, see Alfred Reisch, "Government Wants Negotiated Withdrawal from the Warsaw Pact," *Report on Eastern Europe,* June 8, 1990, pp. 24–34.

22. *Report on Eastern Europe,* November 2, 1990.

23. On the public standing of the Polish army prior to the declaration of martial law, see Edmund Walendowski, *Combat Motivation of the Polish Forces* (London: Macmillan, 1988), especially pp. 19–29 and 56–67.

24. See Bruce D. Porter, "The USSR and Poland on the Road to Martial Law," in Jan B. de Weydenthal et al., eds., *The Polish Drama: 1980–1982* (Lexington, Mass.: Lexington Books, 1983), 101–144.

25. Jan B. de Weydenthal, "Martial Law and the Reliability of the Polish Military," in Nelson, *Soviet Allies,* 226.

26. *Tygodnik Solidarnosc,* August 11, 1989; Warsaw PAP, October 17, 1989 (FBIS); PAP, September 30, 1989 (FBIS); Michael Sadykiewicz, " *'Glasnost'* in the Polish Army: Order of Battle Revealed," RAD Background Report/214, December 5, 1989, *RFER; Gazeta Wyborcza,* October 13–15, 1989.

27. *Zolnierz Wolnosci,* September 16–17, 1989 (FBIS); *Trybuna ludu,* October 20, 1989 (FBIS); Sadykiewicz, " *'Glasnost'* "; Michael Sadykiewicz, "Gorbachev's Impact on the Polish Military," RAD Background Report/109, June 20, 1989, *RFER;* Michael Sadykiewicz and Douglas L. Clarke, "The New Polish Defense Doctrine, A Further Step Toward Sovereignty," *Report on Eastern Europe,* May 4, 1990.

28. *Zolnierz Wolnosci,* September 26, 1989 (FBIS); Anna Sabbat-Swidlicka, "Mazowiecki's Year in Review," *Report on Eastern Europe,* January 4, 1991; Michael Sadykiewicz, "Controlling the Armed Forces in Poland," RAD Background Report/213, December 1, 1989, *RFER.*

29. On the ambiguous feelings Poles have toward Jaruzelski and his rule, see the *New York Times,* December 22, 1990.

30. *RFE/RL Daily Report,* November 9, 1990 and January 5, 1991; Sabbat-Swidlicka, "Mazowiecki's Year," 27; *RFE/RL Daily Report,* April 2, 1991.

31. Anna Sabbat-Swidlicka, "Changes in the Military Prosecution Authorities," *Report on Eastern Europe,* January 11, 1991, pp. 22–23.

32. PAP, October 3, 1990, cited in *RFE/RL Daily Report,* October 4, 1990; *Report on Eastern Europe,* November 23, 1990, p. 35. In January 1991, Deputy Chief of Staff General Franciszek Puchala said the army might shrink to as few as 230,000, with career military forming 50 percent of its ranks. *RFE/RL Daily Report,* January 10, 1991.

33. An interview given to *Gazeta Wyborcza,* cited in *RFE/RL Daily Report,* September 27, 1990.

34. Duncan M. Perry, "A New Military Lobby," *Report on Eastern Europe,* October 5, 1990, p. 1. The entire article (pp. 1–3) is the source for the information in this and the following paragraph.

35. Bucharest Domestic Service, December 22, 1989 (FBIS).

36. Vienna Television Service, December 28, 1989 (FBIS).

37. The general's account of events appeared in *Cuvintul,* no. 5 (February 28, 1990) and is summarized in Michael Shafir, "New Revelations of the Military's Role in Ceausescu's Ouster," *Report on Eastern Europe,* May 11, 1990, pp. 24–26.

38. Shafir, "New Revelations," 25.

39. This event, which has been debated extensively in Romania, is analyzed in great detail in Mihai Sturdza, "The Miners' Crackdown on the Opposition: A Review of the Evidence," *Report on Eastern Europe,* January 11, 1991, pp. 25–32.

40. *RFE/RL Daily Report,* September 27, 1990; November 8 and 9, 1990; January 10, 1991.

41. *RFE/RL Daily Report,* November 30, 1990; *Azi,* December 14, 1990, cited in *RFE/RL Daily Report,* January 11, 1991.

42. Barbara Jelavich, *History of the Balkans: Twentieth Century,* vol. 2 (Cambridge: Cambridge University Press, 1983), 204.

43. On the decline in party membership, see *1990 Yearbook on International Communist Affairs,* 451–452. A good summary of internal developments in 1989 is found on pp. 450–462. In addition to the sources cited, valuable background

information on Yugoslav political developments can be found in articles by RFE researcher Milan Andrejevich: "The Military's Views on Recent Domestic Developments," Yugoslav SR/12, October 23, 1989, *RFER;* "The Military's Role in the Current Constitutional Crisis," *Report on Eastern Europe,* November 9, 1990, pp. 23–27; "The End of an Era, New Beginnings?" *Report on Eastern Europe,* January 4, 1991, pp. 38–44.

44. *New York Times,* July 1, 1991.

45. *Politika* (Belgrade), September 30, 1989, cited in Yugoslav SR/12, October 23, 1989, *RFER.*

46. *RFE/RL Daily Report,* December 3, 1990; *Report on Eastern Europe,* December 14, 1990, p. 44. Retired General Stefan Mirkovic had warned earlier that "any violent or willful attempts to secede will be stopped by force." *Report on Eastern Europe,* November 30, 1990, p. 39.

47. *New York Times,* January 25 and 26, 1991.

48. *RFE/RL Daily Report,* February 25, 1991; March 5, 11, 12, 13, and 15, 1991.

49. *RFE/RL Daily Report,* April 29; May 3 and 8, 1991; *New York Times,* May 8 and 10, 1991.

50. *RFE/RL Daily Report,* May 10, 16, and 21, 1991.

51. *RFE/RL Daily Report,* May 21, 24, 27, and 31, 1991; June 10, 1991; *New York Times,* May 20, 1991; June 6 and 7, 1991.

52. *RFE/RL Daily Report,* June 21 and 25, 1991; July 1, 1991; *New York Times,* June 28 and July 1, 1991.

53. *New York Times,* July 1, 2, 3, and 4, 1991; *RFE/RL Daily Report,* July 3, 1991.

Chapter 3 — Crisis and Adaptation:
The Soviet Armed Forces

1. Jeremy Azrael, *The Soviet Civilian Leadership and the Military High Command, 1976–1986,* R-3251-AF (Santa Monica, Calif.: RAND Corporation, June 1987); Timothy J. Colton, "Perspectives on Civil-Military Relations in the Soviet Union," in Timothy Colton and Thane Gustafson, eds., *Soldiers and the Soviet State: Civil-Military Relations from Brezhnev to Gorbachev* (Princeton, N.J.: Princeton University Press, 1990), 25–29.

2. See Bruce D. Porter, "The Military Abroad: Internal Consequences of External Expansion," in Colton and Gustafson, *Soldiers and the Soviet State*, 305–307.

3. *Pravda,* April 10, 1988.

4. *Sobesednik,* no. 30 (1990), cited in *RFE/RL Daily Report,* August 1, 1990.

5. *RFE/RL Daily Report,* August 20, 1990, citing *The European,* August 17–19, 1990; *RFE/RL Daily Report,* December 17, 1990.

6. Ellen Jones, "Social Change and Civil-Military Relations," in Colton and Gustafson, *Soldiers and the Soviet State,* 239–240.

7. Novosti, September 20, 1990, cited in *RFE/RL Daily Report,* September 21, 1990; *Nedelia,* no. 22 (May 28–June 3, 1990).

8. *Nedelia,* no. 22 (May 28–June 3, 1990); *Soviet/East European Report,* no. 44 (September 10, 1990), citing a report in *Nachalo* (July 1990); *RFE/RL Daily Report,* December 7, 1990.

9. *Der Tagesspiegel,* February 2, 1988; *Frankfurter Allgemeine Zeitung,* July 25, 1987; both cited in "Discipline Problems in the Soviet Group of Forces in the GDR," *RAD Report,* June 29, 1988.

10. *Krasnaia zvezda,* February 17, 1990. For more background on the problem of alcoholism in the Red Army, see Ellen Jones, *Red Army and Society: A Sociology of the Soviet Military* (Boston: Allen & Unwin, 1985), 137–139.

11. Viktor Suvorov, *Inside the Soviet Army* (New York: Berkley, 1984), 262–291, passim. For further information, see also Jones, *Red Army and Society,* 138–141.

12. The reaction to this short story in the Soviet press is described in detail in Stuart Dalrymple, "Bullying in the Soviet Army," *Radio Liberty Research Bulletin,* RL 185/88, April 29, 1988.

13. Yuri I. Deryugin, "Dedovshchina: sotsial'no-psikhologicheskii analiz yavleniia" (Military hazing: A socio-psychological analysis), *Psikhologicheskii zhurnal,* no. 1 (1990): 112.

14. The Yazov statement is from the *International Herald Tribune,* May 9, 1990. For sociological analysis of the relation-

ship between ethnic problems and *dedovshchina,* see Deryugin, "Dedovshchina," 113–115.

15. *Argumenty i fakty,* no. 8 (May 1990).

16. *Krasnaia zvezda,* October 13, 1989.

17. This charge was first raised by demonstrators at Gorki Park in June 1990. See *RFE/RL Daily Report,* June 5, 1990 and August 10, 1990. The charge was subsequently repeated by *Vecherniaia Moskva,* July 20, 1990, and *Komsomolskaia pravda,* August 2, 1990. See also *Soviet/East European Report* 7, no. 44 (September 10, 1990), citing a report in *Nachalo* (July 1990).

18. *RFE/RL Daily Report,* November 16, 1990. For further details on this decree and on the efforts of Soviet private organizations to redress the problem, see Rosamund Shreeves, "Mothers against the Draft: Women's Activism in the USSR," *Report on the USSR,* September 21, 1990, pp. 3–8; and Stephen Foye, " 'Noncombat Deaths': Gorbachev's Decree Reflects Army Woes," *Report on the USSR,* September 21, 1990, pp. 1–3.

19. The Yazov quotations are from *Krasnaia zvezda,* December 25, 1988 and August 19, 1990. Figures on military casualties are from *Krasnaia zvezda,* July 12, 1990. This article claimed that as of July, 189 Soviet officers had suffered injuries and 21 had died in 1990 from attacks by "hooligans."

20. *Pravda,* November 25, 1987; *Molod Ukrainy,* January 15, 1987; *Krasnaia zvezda,* December 5, 1985; *Krasnaia zvezda,* July 11, 1986; *Pravda vostoka,* February 21, 1987.

21. *Krasnaia zvezda,* December 15, 1988; *Komsmolskoe znamia,* December 4, 1988. See also Kathleen Mihalisko, "Report from Kiev University on Future of Student Military Obligations," *Report on the USSR,* January 27, 1989.

22. See *Krasnaia zvezda,* August 13 and 31, 1989; *Izvestia,* September 13, 1989; see also Stephen Foye, "Students and the Soviet Military," *Report on the USSR,* September 29, 1989.

23. *Komsomolskaia pravda,* November 21, 1989; *RFE/RL Daily Report,* July 17, 1991.

24. The Central Television report of June 10 and TASS report of June 11 are cited in Stephen Foye, "Statistics Show

Low Military Draft Turnout in Republics," *Report on the USSR,*
July 18, 1990.

25. *International Herald Tribune,* September 30–October
1, 1989.

26. *Washington Post,* September 28, 1990.

27. Cited in *RFE/RL Daily Report,* October 16, 1990.
Additional information in this paragraph is from *Krasnaia
zvezda,* October 3, 1990, and *Interfax,* October 3, 1990,
reported by Agence France Presse (AFP) and cited in *RFE/RL
Daily Report,* October 4, 1990. Agence France Presse reported
in January 1991 that the Soviet Defense Ministry claimed that
only 78.8 percent of conscripts had appeared for the fall draft,
and only 10 percent from Georgia, 12.5 percent from
Lithuania, and under 30 percent in Estonia and Latvia; see
AFP, cited in *RFE/RL Daily Report,* January 8, 1991. For more
recent figures suggesting the problem has continued in 1991,
see *RFE/RL Daily Report,* March 4, 1991.

28. Krivosheev published these figures in "Na sluzhbe
otechestvu," April 14, 1991, cited in *RFE/RL Daily Report,*
April 17, 1991. Earlier in the year he told a Soviet television
audience that 84 percent of the fall draft quota had been met.
RFE/RL Daily Report, January 28, 1991. On the low draft
turnout in Moldavia, see *RFE/RL Daily Report,* June 7, 1991,
which quotes the Moldavian press agency, Moldovapress, as
claiming that in the spring 1991 call-up, only 5,000 of 11,000
eligible Moldavians reported for duty, less than half of those
eligible and a further decline from the figures Novosti had
reported for the fall 1990 draft.

29. *Krasnaia zvezda,* June 22, 1990. Boiko also criticized
the "anti-army syndrome" of the Soviet liberal press.

30. *RFE/RL Daily Report,* January 14, 1991.

31. Milan Hauner and Alexander Rahr, "New Chief of
Soviet General Staff Appointed," *Radio Liberty Research
Bulletin,* RL 546/88, December 16, 1988.

32. *Izvestia,* September 16, 1989.

33. *Izvestia,* February 22, 1990. See also an earlier article
by Moiseev, "Eshche raz o prestizhe armii" (Once more on the
army's prestige), *Kommunist vooruzhennykh sil,* no. 13
(1989). For more information on military opposition to defense cuts, see John Tedstrom, "Military Opposition to Cuts in

Defense Expenditure," *Report on the USSR,* March 16, 1990, pp. 3–5.

34. *Kommunist vooruzhennykh sil,* no. 1 (1990).

35. *Kommunist vooruzhennykh sil,* no. 3 (1990): 30–36.

36. Central Television, September 15, 1990, cited in *RFE/RL Daily Report,* September 17, 1990.

37. *Pravda,* June 11, 1989; *Izvestia,* June 8, 1989; *Jane's Soviet Intelligence Review,* March 1990; *RFE/RL Daily Report,* November 29, 1990.

38. *Soviet Military Power,* 34; "Estimates of Soviet Defense Expenditures," Radio Liberty Research (RLR)/Backgrounder, May 5, 1988; John Tedstrom, "The Economics of Soviet Defense Spending," *Radio Liberty Research Bulletin,* RL Supplement 4/88, August 15, 1988; *Novoe vremia,* no. 26 (1989); Alexei Kireev, "Skol'ko tratit na oborny?" (How much for defense?), *Ogonek,* no. 7 (May 6–13, 1989); Yuri Kornilov, "Sekrety Pariteta" (Secrets of parity), *Ogonek,* no. 15 (1990); "Stavka na kachestvo," *Moskovskie novosti,* no. 11, March 18, 1990.

39. *RFE/RL Daily Report,* October 1, 1990; *Trud* of the same day reported Deputy Defense Minister Vitalii Shabanov as calling for the somewhat lower figure of 422 military plants converted by 1995.

40. *Soviet Military Power; Komsomolskaia pravda,* November 29, 1990. The normally liberal newspaper even argued that conversion would undermine "the only sound sector of the economy."

41. *Pod znamenem leninizma,* no. 2 (1990): 32–36, cited in Stephen Foye, "Rumblings in the Soviet Armed Forces," *Report on the USSR,* March 16, 1990.

42. Gromov ran an article highly critical of the liberal media in *Sovetskaia Rossiia,* November 15, 1989. *Komsomolskaia pravda* responded on November 25 with an open letter to the general challenging the substance of his criticisms. There was also an exchange between *Komsomolskaia pravda* and Colonel General Grigorii Krivosheev; see *Krasnaia zvezda,* July 12, 1990.

43. *La Repubblica,* November 22, 1989, cited in FBIS, November 30, 1989.

44. *Krasnaia zvezda,* December 31, 1989; January 7 and 11, 1990.

45. *Sovetskaia Rossiia,* June 21, 1990; cited in Stephen Foye, "Military Hard-Liner Condemns 'New Thinking' in Security Policy," *Report on the USSR,* July 13, 1990, pp. 4–6.

46. *Izvestia,* June 20, 1990; Central Television, "Vremya," June 23, 1990; and *Pravda,* June 26, 1990; all cited in Foye, "Military Hard-Liner." Rumors later spread (*Financial Times,* July 28, 1990) that Makashov had been banished to service in Iraq (!), but he reappeared in a *Krasnaia zvezda* interview of July 29, still identified as commander of the Volga-Urals district and still critical of defense cuts and of the liberal media. *RFE/RL Daily Report,* August 2, 1990.

47. Stephen Foye, "Defense Issues at the Party Congress," *Report on the USSR,* July 27, 1990, pp. 1–5.

48. TASS, September 12, 1990, cited in *RFE/RL Daily Report,* September 13, 1990.

49. A profile of Filatov appears in the *New York Times,* January 7, 1991.

50. *Literaturnaia Rossiia,* January 5, 1990; for more detail see Vera Tolz and Elizabeth Teague, "Prokhanov Warns of Collapse of Soviet Empire," *Report on the USSR,* February 9, 1990.

51. *Voenno-istoricheskii zhurnal,* no. 4 (1989): 4, cited in Mikhail Tsypkin, "Karem Rash: An Ideologue of Military Power," *Report on the USSR,* August 3, 1990, pp. 8–11.

52. *New York Times,* December 24, 1990. Yazov publicly disassociated himself from these two "Black Colonels" in an interview published in *Sobesednik,* no. 8 (1991), cited in *RFE/RL Daily Report,* March 5, 1991.

53. *New York Times,* July 19, 1990.

54. The letter was published in *Ekho Litvy,* July 18, 1990; cited in *RFE/RL Daily Report,* July 19, 1990.

55. *RFE/RL Daily Report,* July 26, 1990.

56. *RFE/RL Daily Report,* July 26, 1990; July 27, 1990; August 1, 1990; TASS, September 12, 1990, cited twice in *RFE/RL Daily Report,* September 13, 1990; October 11, 1990.

57. *Krasnaia zvezda,* August 19, 1990.

58. *Washington Post,* September 28, 1990. The Soviet Defense Ministry on October 3 denied that any weapons had

been moved. *Krasnaia zvezda,* October 3, 1990. See also Alexander Rahr and R. Alex Bryan, "Concern over Security of Soviet Nuclear Arms," *Report on the USSR,* October 12, 1990, pp. 6–7.

59. The most complete account is in *Krasnaia zvezda,* November 15, 1990; other accounts were carried in *Izvestia,* November 15, 1990 and the *Washington Post,* November 16, 1990; for summaries see *RFE/RL Daily Report,* November 15, 1990 and Stephen Foye, "Gorbachev, the Army and the Union," *Report on the USSR,* December 7, 1990.

60. Radio Moscow, October 10, 1990, cited in *RFE/RL Daily Report,* October 11, 1990; Central Television, November 25, 1990, cited in *RFE/RL Daily Report,* November 26, 1990.

61. TASS, October 17, 1990, cited in *RFE/RL Daily Report,* October 18, 1990; and Radio Riga, November 26, 1990, cited in *RFE/RL Daily Report,* November 27, 1990.

62. *New York Times,* November 28, 1990; TASS, November 27, 1990, cited in Foye, "Gorbachev, the Army, and the Union," 1. Yazov also told *Komsomolskaia pravda* on December 1 that Baltic authorities were threatening the army and that Soviet troops would seize local supply facilities if necessary. *RFE/RL Daily Report,* December 3, 1990.

63. Radio Moscow, November 28, 1990, cited in *RFE/RL Daily Report,* November 30, 1990; *Izvestia,* November 29, 1990; TASS, November 23, 1990, cited in *RFE/RL Daily Report,* November 24, 1990.

64. On these events, see *Pravda,* December 3, 1990; *RFE/RL Daily Report,* December 3 and 4, 1990; Stephen Foye, "The Case for a Coup: Gorbachev or the Generals?" *Report on the USSR,* January 11, 1991, p. 4.

65. *New York Times,* December 21, 1990; *RFE/RL Daily Report,* January 2 and 3, 1991. For further background on the January crackdown, see John B. Dunlop, "Crackdown," *National Interest* (Spring 1991): 24–32.

66. *New York Times,* February 5 and 6, 1991; *RFE/RL Daily Report,* February 5, 1991.

67. *RFE/RL Daily Report,* February 27, 1991; March 5, 8, and 15, 1991; April 4, 1991.

68. *Molodaia gvardiia,* no. 5, 1991, cited in *RFE/RL Daily Report,* June 18, 1991; *New York Times,* June 28, 1991; *RFE/*

RL Daily Report, April 22, 1991 and June 24, 1991. The speeches of the "triumvirate" were carried by *Sovetskaia Rossiia,* June 27, 1991 (see FBIS, same date).

69. *Sovetskaia Rossiia,* July 23, 1991, carried the letter signed by the 12 hard-line critics of the regime.

70. *RFE/RL Daily Report,* August 13 and 14, 1991.

71. *New York Times,* August 17, 1991.

72. In September 1990, the transfer of an airborne regiment from Ryazan to Moscow and other troop movements around the capital city led to a spate of rumors about an impending military coup. Contradictory accounts about the purpose of the deployments only fueled the rumors: the troops were said by the Ministry of Defense to be preparing for the traditional November 7 parade; the commander of Soviet airborne troops said they were engaged in a classified exercise; troops sent to Ryazan to replace the transferred units were said to be helping with the potato harvest but were seen dressed in full combat gear. No concrete evidence ever surfaced that these troop movements had any political objective or that they were not sanctioned by civilian authorities. But they led two liberal Soviet publications—*Moskovskie novosti* and *Komsomolskaia pravda*—to express open concern about the prospect for a military coup. Yeltsin voiced concern about the mission of the airborne units, while Colonel Vilen Martirosian, a people's deputy from the Interregional Group, published a letter in *Moskovskie novosti* co-signed by 47 parliamentary colleagues warning of a possible coup. On September 19, Defense Minister Yazov felt obliged to make an official statement on national television denying reports of an impending coup. See *Jane's Soviet Intelligence Review,* November 1990, pp. 525–526; *RFE/RL Daily Report,* September 17 and 20, 1990; *Sovetskaia Rossiia,* September 27 and 30, 1990.

73. Information about the coup is taken from the *New York Times* of August 20, 21, 22, and 23, 1991 and from *RFE/RL Daily Report,* of the same dates, except where otherwise noted.

74. See *Krasnaia zvezda,* August 27, 1991, cited in *RFE/RL Daily Report,* August 28, 1991.

75. The Ogarkov quote is from *Vsegda v gotovnosti k zashchite Otechestva* (Always ready for defense of the Father-

land) (Moscow: USSR Ministry of Defense, 1982), 59.

76. An excellent article on the reform objectives of the Soviet officer corps is Ilana Kass and Fred Clark Boli, "The Soviet Military's Transcentury Agenda," *Comparative Strategy* 9, no. 4 (1990): 319–333.

77. Ogarkov spoke before a plenum of the All-Union Council of War and Labor Veterans. TASS, November 29, 1990, reported in *RFE/RL Daily Report,* November 30, 1990.

78. For recent representative examples of their thinking, voiced at nearly the same time, see *Krasnaia zvezda,* November 18, 1990; Novosti, September 13, 1990, cited in *RFE/RL Daily Report,* September 14, 1990. Yazov has been on record since at least early 1989 as opposing proposals for reforming the Soviet conscription system; see *Krasnaia zvezda,* April 13, 1989.

79. *Reuter,* August 13, 1990, cited in *RFE/RL Daily Report,* August 13, 1990; *Liberation,* July 15, 1990, cited in *RFE/RL Daily Report,* September 14, 1990.

80. *Krasnaia zvezda,* July 20, 1990; *Izvestia,* July 18, 1990. Shlyaga insisted that political workers defend Lenin in a speech reported by TASS on September 4, 1990, cited in *RFE/RL Daily Report,* September 5, 1990. On Lobov's views, see "Voennaia reforma: tseli, printsipy, soderzhanie" (Military reform: goals, principles, content), *Kommunist,* no. 13 (1990): 14–22, and "Predvedenie" (Foresight), *Znamia,* no. 2 (1990): 170–182. See also Stephen Foye, "Hard-Liner Calls for Military Reform," *Report on the USSR,* October 26, 1990, pp. 6–8. Shaposhnikov was interviewed in *Izvestia,* August 13, 1990.

81. TASS, January 14, 1991, cited in *RFE/RL Daily Report,* January 15, 1991.

82. Stephen Foye, "Lopatin on Party Control of the Armed Forces," *Report on the USSR,* September 14, 1990, pp. 3–5. Smirnov's description of treatment by the mainline officers appeared in *Moskovskie novosti,* no. 36 (1990). A recent military critique of Lopatin can be found in *Krasnaia zvezda,* January 17, 1991.

83. *RFE/RL Daily Report,* May 14, 1991. The Supreme Soviet also reduced naval service from three years to two years, bringing it in line with the other services. On the issue of a professional army, see *Krasnaia zvezda,* August 20, 1990;

Robert Arnett and Mary Fitzgerald, "Is the Soviet Military Leadership Yielding on an All-Volunteer Army?" *Report on the USSR*, March 30, 1990, pp. 3–5.

84. TASS, September 4, 1990, cited in *RFE/RL Daily Report*, September 5, 1990. For additional background, see Stephen Foye, "Gorbachev and Depoliticization of the Army," *Report on the USSR*, September 14, 1990, pp. 1–3.

85. Gorbachev's decree is found in TASS International Service, June 24, 1991 (FBIS, June 25, 1991). Yeltsin's decree was carried on Radio Moscow, July 20, 1991 (FBIS, July 22, 1991).

86. Mark Galeotti, "The Soviet Army's New Interest in Imperial Traditions," *Report on the USSR*, December 28, 1990, pp. 8–9.

87. Novosti, October 23, 1990, cited in *RFE/RL Daily Report*, October 24, 1990.

Chapter 4 — Crisis and Reaction: Socialist Armies Outside Europe

1. On China's internal problems in general, see Michael D. Swaine, "China Faces the 1990s: A System in Crisis," *Problems of Communism* 39 (May–June 1990): 20–35.

2. The speech can be found in the *South China Morning Post*, June 20, 1989 (FBIS). See *Far Eastern Economic Review*, July 29, 1990, for an analysis of the speech.

3. Paul H. B. Godwin, "Civil-Military Relations in China: The Guerrilla Experience," *Studies in Comparative Communism* 11, no. 3 (Autumn 1978): 268.

4. Ibid., 265–266, 273–277.

5. Ellis Joffe, "The Political Role of the Chinese Army: Overview and Evaluation," in Yu-ming Shaw, ed., *Power and Policy in the PRC* (Boulder, Colo.: Westview Press, 1985), 161. See also pp. 159–163.

6. Harry Harding, *Organizing China: The Problem of Bureaucracy 1949–1976* (Stanford, Calif.: Stanford University Press, 1981), 300. Civil-military relations during the Cultural Revolution were quite complex and cannot possibly be reviewed in any detail here. For a good summary of the period and of the PLA's political role generally, see Parris H. Chang,

"Changing Patterns of Military Roles in Chinese Politics," in William W. Whitson, ed., *The Military and Political Power in China in the 1970s* (New York: Praeger, 1972), 47–70.

7. Joffe, "Political Role of the Chinese Army," 157–159.

8. On this point, see Edward L. Dreyer, "Military Continuities: The PLA and Imperial China," in Whitson, *Military and Political Power in China,* 4–7.

9. Except where otherwise noted, this and the following account of events are taken from the following sources: *Far Eastern Economic Review,* June 8, 14, and 22, 1989 and July 29, 1989; *Keesing's Record of World Events,* May and June 1989; Far Eastern Economic Review, *Asia 1990 Yearbook,* 106–116; *1990 Yearbook on International Communist Affairs,* 182–191; *Asiaweek,* December 22–29, 1989; Bernard Gwertzman and Michael T. Kaufmann, eds., *The Collapse of Communism* (New York: Random House, 1990), 41–109 (a collection of dispatches that appeared in the *New York Times*); *Inside China Mainland* 11, no. 8 (August 1989). The last source contains the texts of Li Peng's May 19 speech, the Martial Law Order from the State Council, and the three related orders from the Beijing city government issued on May 20. I have also benefited from comments by Gerrit W. Gong and from his superb first-hand account, "Tiananmen: Causes and Consequences," *Washington Quarterly* 13, no. 1 (Winter 1990): 79–95.

10. See June Teufel Dreyer, "The People's Liberation Army and the Power Struggle of 1989," *Problems of Communism* 38 (September–October 1989): 42–43. These reports mostly came out of Hong Kong and their accuracy cannot be confirmed.

11. Ian Wilson and You Ji, "Leadership by 'Lines,' " 38–42; Dreyer, "People's Liberation Army."

12. *Asiaweek*, December 22–29, 1989.

13. Beijing television announced on June 6 that 300 persons had died as a result of the "counterrevolutionary rebellion," most of them soldiers. Estimates of the number of student and citizen casualties range from 200 to over 5,000. *Asiaweek,* December 22–29, 1989 claims that the higher figures are definitely exaggerated and that the government's figure may be closer to the mark than previously thought.

14. Gwertzman and Kaufmann, *Collapse of Communism*, 92. According to the *Far Eastern Economic Review*, June 22, 1989, the killing of unarmed civilians "irrevocably alienated" the PLA from the populace.

15. These reports are summarized in "Tiananmen: What Did Happen?" *Asiaweek*, December 22–29, 1989, pp. 30–32. See also *Keesing's Record of World Events*, June 1989, p. 36721.

16. *Far Eastern Economic Review*, June 14, 1989.

17. Ibid., June 29, 1989.

18. Swaine, "China Faces the 1990s," 27.

19. Xinhua Domestic Service, November 15, 1989 (FBIS). Emphasis added.

20. Ibid.

21. See, for example, the article "Thoughts on Education in National Defense After the Quelling of the Rebellion," in *Remnin Ribao*, September 15, 1989 (FBIS) and a separate report on the work of the Discipline Inspection Commission in the same publication, September 16, 1989 (FBIS). See also the speech by Yang Baibing on political work in the military *Liberation Army Daily*, July 25, 1989, cited in *Inside China Mainland* (November 1989): 20–21. On the military education program, see Stephan Uhalloy, Jr., "China," in *1990 Yearbook on International Communist Affairs*, 191. Another source of concern during this period was a rise in draft-dodging. See *Liberation Army Daily*, July 27, 1989, cited in *Inside China Mainland* (November 1989): 25.

22. Xinhua Domestic Service, December 17, 1989.

23. *Far Eastern Economic Review*, June 14, 1990.

24. Deng Xiaoping stepped down as head of the Central Military Commission toward the end of 1989. His replacement was Jiang Zemin, the general secretary of the CPC, who had replaced Zhao Ziyang in June. Jiang's combination of positions would seem to make him a likely successor to Deng. His lack of any known military experience, however, would work against him in any power struggle and could cause the PLA to view his prospective accession negatively. The PLA is known to advocate appointing a military officer as head of the CMC.

25. Cited in Far Eastern Economic Review, *Asia 1990 Yearbook*, 246.

26. Gareth Porter, "The Politics of 'Renovation' in Vietnam," *Problems of Communism* 39 (May–June 1990): 72–88.

27. Douglas Pike, *PAVN: People's Army of Vietnam* (Novato, Calif.: Presidio Press, 1986), 145–146. On the relationship between the PAVN and the Party, see also pp. 147–180 and 284–288.

28. Far Eastern Economic Review, *Asia 1990 Yearbook*, 246.

29. Ibid., 241.

30. On these points, see Douglas Pike, "Vietnam," in *1990 Yearbook on International Communist Affairs*, 287.

31. Far Eastern Economic Review, *Asia 1990 Yearbook*, 151.

32. *1990 Yearbook on International Communist Affairs*, 223.

33. Far Eastern Economic Review, *Asia 1990 Yearbook*, 151–152.

34. *Keesing's Record of World Events*, May 1990, p. 37455.

35. William M. LeoGrande, "Civil-Military Relations in Cuba: Party Control and Political Socialization," *Studies in Comparative Communism* 11, no. 3 (Autumn 1978): 279.

36. Raúl Castro admitted in 1966 that military officers were resisting the creation of any kind of political apparatus in the army. LeoGrande, "Civil-Military Relations," 285.

37. *Granma Weekly Review* (English edition), December 17, 1989.

38. This speech as well as a detailed chronology and transcript of the trial may be found in a special issue of *Cuba Update* (Fall 1989).

39. *Wall Street Journal*, September 25, 1989 and June 29, 1989; *Christian Science Monitor*, June 21, 1989; *Newsweek*, August 7, 1989.

40. This theory is summarized in detail in *1990 Yearbook on International Communist Affairs*, 77–78. See also pp. 75–78 for more details on the Ochoa trial and its broader implications.

41. *Granma Weekly Review* (English edition), October 1, 1989; *Latin American Regional Reports Caribbean*, April 5, 1990.

42. George Volsky, "Cuba," in *1990 Yearbook on International Communist Affairs*, 78. *Granma*, November 5, 1989; *Latin American Regional Reports Caribbean*, November 8,

1990. *Granma Weekly Review* (English edition), March 5, 1990, cited the figure of 31,434 soldiers returning from abroad as of that date. *Granma* in several issues glorified the achievements of the overseas contingents; see issues of September 11, 1989; October 8, 1989; and December 17, 1989. The Western scholar quoted is Michael J. Mazarr, "Prospects for Revolution in Post-Castro Cuba," *Journal of Inter-American Studies and World Affairs* (Winter 1989): 79; the entire article, pp. 61–90, is a good review of the internal problems facing Cuban society.

43. Information on Nicaragua is taken from *Facts on File Yearbook* 50 (1990): 150, 297, 991–992; and from the *Washington Post,* June 19 and 23, 1991 and July 25, 1991. Information on Angola is from *Keesing's Record of World Events,* April 1991, p. 38133, and May 1991, p. 38180; and from the *Washington Post,* June 17, 1991. Information on Ethiopia is from *Africa Report* (July–August 1991): 5–6; *1990 Yearbook on International Communist Affairs,* 14–15; *Keesing's Record of World Events,* May 1989, pp. 36646–36647; June 1989, p. 36728; February 1991, p. 37996; May 1991, pp. 38174–38175.